THIS BOOK is to
commemorate the issuance of the
official Cherokee medal
November 15, 1973
and is limited to 15,000 copies

No. _10225_

N.M.Keeler

WARS AND RUMORS OF WARS — a painting of a council of Cherokee leaders by Cherokee-Creek artist Joan Hill.

THE
CHEROKEE
PEOPLE

by Earl Boyd Pierce
and
Rennard Strickland

Scientific Editors: Henry F. Dobyns and W. David Baird
General Editor: John I. Griffin

PUBLISHED BY INDIAN TRIBAL SERIES / PHOENIX

FOREWORD

I T IS A REAL THRILL to have the opportunity to place a few words in the Foreword of this book. For the past forty years I have been involved in Indian work with practically all of the tribes in the United States. Over this period of time it has been increasingly obvious to me that one of the greatest obstacles the North American Indian meets is the fact that he is very ignorant of his heritage and has accepted the general concept that he is a second class citizen. I have never felt that money as payments per se would ever be the answer to the Indian problem in this country. We have seen two instances that tend to confirm this viewpoint: the Osage Indians of Oklahoma, with the tremendous wealth that came to them from oil operations on the land that they owned the mineral rights to, and also the Klamath Tribe which had tremendous holdings in the valuable lumber resources of the Northwest and was one of those tribes that experienced the termination of the federal government's responsibility to an Indian tribe.

In both cases, the fullblood Indians benefited very little because up to the fairly recent past the government has only been a custodian of Indian property and disregarded completely the necessity to develop the human resources. These two tribes were not prepared to cope with the sudden wealth that came upon them. This history, so ably written by Mr. Earl Boyd Pierce and Dr. Rennard Strickland, brings out clearly that the Cherokee Indians were anxious to develop human resources, and, more important, did so when they operated independently of the federal government. I believe that our Indian people reading this book will develop a pride in their heritage and generate confidence in their ability to overcome the obstacles of living in a culture foreign to their own.

I am also grateful that two such dedicated men would join in the co-authorship of *The Cherokee People*. Too many times in the past books and stories have been written about the Cherokees with very little, if any, knowledge of their background and history.

I enthusiastically recommend this book to all of our people with the hope that it will do for them as it did for me — remind them that we are a dynamic people.

W. W. Keeler
Principal Chief of the Cherokee Nation
Bartlesville, Oklahoma
August 25, 1973

INTRODUCTION

THIS BRIEF AND INTERESTING ACCOUNT of the history and present achievements of the Cherokee Nation of the State of Oklahoma demonstrates what an Indian tribe presently can do toward emancipating its people from the paternalism of the United States under our free enterprise system. This study of the Cherokee Nation is written by Earl Boyd Pierce, Esquire, an enrolled Cherokee Indian and General Counsel of the Cherokee Nation, who was born and raised in the Cherokee country and who has experienced these late developments and helped to accomplish them. His co-author is Doctor Rennard Strickland, a native Oklahoman, Law Professor at Tulsa University, Tulsa, Oklahoma, and an historian of note.

Before and during the historic period, the Cherokee people developed a culture which was suited to the environment in which they lived. Owning a vast territory in what is now the southeastern United States, they lived a hardy life based upon hunting and agricultural pursuits. Game and fish were plentiful in the virgin forests and streams, and crops planted in the rich soils produced in abundance.

This way of life was completely disrupted by the advent of the white man, who took from the Cherokees their ancestral lands, forests and streams, and forced them to remove to new lands in the West, then known as Indian Territory, now eastern Oklahoma. Promises were made to the Cherokees that in the West they could forever pursue their own way of life free from interference from the white man. Treaties guaranteed to the Cherokees the right of self-government, that no Territory or State would be created out of their lands without their consent, and granted fee simple title to their western domain.

The Cherokees were reluctant to give up their ancestral homes in the East, but eventually were driven by military force to new homes in the West. There they again built their homes, set up their government patterned after our own constitutional form, and for a time were secure in their new environment.

Because the United States failed in its treaty promises of protection, in the 1860's the Cherokees were again forced to rebuild their homes devastated by the Civil War, and again to rehabilitate themselves in their new territory.

In 1893, the government again surrounded their country, and made the same demand for their lands as was made in the East, and forced agreements upon the Cherokees under which they were required to give up their tribal title to lands, allot their lands to members of the tribe, and give up most of the functions of their own government, in order to make way for the creation of the new State of Oklahoma. Thus, a wholly new concept of land ownership was forced upon them.

In 1946, when Congress passed the Indian Claims Commission Act authorizing the Indian tribes to bring suits against the United States for wrongs done by the government in its dealings with the Indian tribes, the Cherokee Nation had no tribal funds to finance the litigation. Counsel accepted employment to prosecute its claims upon a contingent fee basis. The successful outcome of this litigation proved the initial means for revitalizing the Cherokee Nation, and inspired in its leaders new hope for the greater advancement of the Cherokee people. The litigation also settled finally all claims asserted by the United States against the Cherokee Nation in the form of gratuity offsets totaling $2,239,577.52. As a consequence, the present assets of the Cherokee Nation are now free of all encumbrances. Blessed with good leadership, these new tribal programs have blossomed into the present accomplishments which are set forth in the account which follows.

Paul M. Niebell

Washington, D. C.
September 1, 1973

ABOUT THE PRINCIPAL CHIEF

THE SON OF ENROLLED CHEROKEES, William Wayne Keeler was born on April 5, 1908, at Dalhart, Texas. He attended public schools in Bartlesville, Oklahoma, and in 1926 entered the University of Kansas where he earned a degree in engineering. Working part time for Phillips Petroleum Company during his early school years, Keeler joined that corporation full time in 1928. His dedication, expertise, and leadership qualities brought him rapid promotion, and in 1951 he was elected vice-president of the executive department and to the board of directors of the company. By 1968, he had become chairman of the board of directors and chief executive officer. After years of meritorious service, he resigned the latter post on January 1, 1973, and upon reaching normal retirement age resigned as chairman on April 1, 1973.

Through the course of his affiliation with Phillips and during a very active civic career, Keeler has remained faithful to his Indian heritage. He was founder and is trustee of the Cherokee Foundation. In 1949, President Truman appointed him Principal Chief of the Cherokees, a trust to which he was elected in 1971 following the first tribal election held since Oklahoma statehood. In addition to his interest in the welfare of the Cherokees, Keeler has also

W. W. KEELER, PRINCIPAL CHIEF

worked to advance the cause of all Indians. He has served on the Commission on the Rights, Liberties, and Responsibilities of the American Indian sponsored by the Fund of the Republic. In February, 1961, he was named by Secretary of the Interior Stewart L. Udall to head a task force to develop plans for the reorganization of the Bureau of Indian Affairs. The following year he was appointed to a three-man task force to study operations of that Bureau in Alaska. In 1964, he chaired the United States delegation to the Inter-American Indian Conference at Quito, Ecuador.

Keeler's service as chief, Indian leader, and industrialist has brought him numerous honors. Not only has he been twice honored with the All-American Indian Award, but he has also received the Indian Achievement Award of the Indian Council Fire and been elected to the Oklahoma Hall of Fame. In addition to a host of civic awards, he holds honorary doctorate degrees from at least four institutions of higher education.

Chief Keeler and his wife, the former Ruby Hamilton, maintain a residence in Bartlesville, Oklahoma. They are the parents of three sons — William, Bradford and Richard.

T HE CHEROKEES ARE NOW and have been for 150 years a literate people. Today hundreds are college graduates, and many may be found in almost every vocation and calling in the United States. Like other Americans some have achieved national and international fame, including the venerated Sequoyah, Robert L. Owen and Will Rogers. Other Cherokees are moderately rich; some are fairly well to do; but the vast majority are no different than most American citizens in affluence and ability.

A large portion of the nation's fullblood citizens who admirably embrace the ancient, traditional religion of their fathers has experienced economic difficulty. Widespread concern for the economic and educational opportunities of these fullbloods has inspired many to follow the objectives of the "revitalized" Cherokee Nation established by two dedicated leaders — the late Principal Chief J. Bartley Milam (1884-1949) and the current elected principal chief, W. W. Keeler. Both chiefs, men of excep-

WILL ROGERS, 1879-1935, greatest of all American humorists. His family was one of the most important and distinguished in Cherokee history. See page 89 for biography.

ROBERT LATHAM OWEN, 1856-1947, U. S. Senator, Co-author of Federal Reserve Bank Act of 1913. See page 90 for biography.

tional talent and substance who have spurned any form of remuneration for thirty years and more, have rendered signal and totally unselfish service to the Cherokee people.

Economic opportunities of the cherished full-blood segment of the Cherokee Nation have steadily improved. Almost everyone now concedes that, despite a few unseemly distractions, the Cherokees are pleasantly witnessing the birth of a "New Golden Age," with the brightest gleam and promise of their age-old "Eternal Fire." The federal government, the State of Oklahoma, and the vast majority of its citizens have been worthy partners in this prideful undertaking.

THE EARLY CHEROKEES

There were times when the future of the Cherokee people did not appear so bright. Indeed, it is said that "The Death Song of the Ancient Cherokees" was an Eighteenth Century "air brought to England from America by a Gentleman, long conversant with the Indian Tribe." The lyrics lamented and prophesied the inevitable passing, the sunset and fading lights of tribal glory.

The Sun sets in Night, and the Stars Shun the Day, But Glory Remains when their lights fade away, Begin ye Tormentors, your threats are in vain, For the Son of ALKNOMOOK shall never complain.

4

I go to the Land where my Father is gone,
His Ghost shall rejoice in the Fame of his
Son! Death comes like a Friend, he relieves
me from Pain, and thy Son, O! ALKNO-
MOOK has scorned to complain.

To the intelligent European observer, it appeared that the Cherokees were doomed. Cherokee "Kings" had visited royal society and the people of England had taken the native visitors to their hearts. Yet they were sure that what had happened to the Indians of New England and many other tribes along the southeastern coast of America would happen to the Cherokees. This tribe, most felt, was at the twilight of its civilization and would soon be destroyed.

By all odds the Cherokees should have disappeared. The Cherokee people, however, did not die. They not only survived, but they actually prospered. From a people teetering dangerously close to extinction in the Eighteenth Century, the Cherokees became the most powerful and most influential tribe in the U. S. in the Nineteenth Century. Today, their status is equal to that of any people on earth.

The survival of the Cherokees was indeed a miracle. As the early inhabitants of the vast Appalachian mountain ranges, these tribesmen stood astride the battleground for colonial supremacy and squarely in the path of western settlement. Repeated colonial wars were costly, cutting tribal ranks again and again.

"I left the people," the frontier artist George Catlin later wrote of the Cherokees, "with a heavy heart, wishing them success and the blessings of the Great Spirit who alone can avert the doom that would almost seem to be fixed." Catlin, like so many of the great men of the Nineteenth Century, was moved by the Cherokee story — the story of a southeastern tribe whose members, before being driven west, became civilized in order to preserve themselves as a distinct people. The miraculous success of the Cherokees in propelling themselves into American civilization prompted no less worldly an observer than Alexis de Tocqueville to conclude in his *Democracy in America* that "the success of the Cherokees proves that the Indians are capable of civilization."

The magnitude of the Cherokee success in fashioning a constitutional government, inventing a syllabary, establishing a newspaper, opening free public schools, and creating a prosperous farmer and merchant class may blind one to the fact that the Cherokees were not always regarded as a people so civilized. The ancient Cherokees were respected warriors and hunters who conceived battle to be the "beloved occupation" and who won and held their mountain terrain by skill in the military arts.

When Hernando de Soto, the famous Spanish

explorer, came among them in the 1540's, the Cherokees had already begun to extend their influence over large parts of Kentucky, Tennessee, North and South Carolina, Virginia, Alabama and Georgia. By 1700, the Cherokee Nation controlled over 70,000,000 acres of well-watered hunting domain. English and French explorers who ventured there after de Soto described the eastern reaches of the Cherokee homeland as a paradise.

Even in 1540 the origin of Cherokee civilization was so distant that the Cherokees knew only the legends of their past. The historic facts were lost in the mist of antiquity. A few students of their culture believe that they came from Mexico, and some that they came from the islands of the Indies. An even larger group contends that they came from the north, gradually migrating south from the Iroquois. The Walum Olum of the Delaware records a battle with the Cherokees near the Ohio River. Based upon linguistic evidence, the Iroquois origin view prevails.

James Adair, an early English trader, believed the Cherokees to be one of the lost tribes of Israel. Although the "lost tribe theory" has long been discredited, the kinship is true in spirit although not in fact. The Cherokees, like the children of Israel, have been driven before their enemies. They have built and have been destroyed. They have built again to be destroyed

7

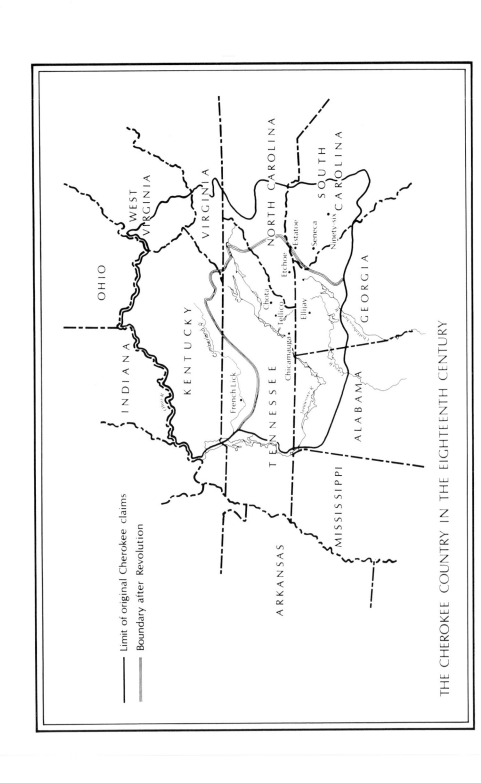

THE CHEROKEE COUNTRY IN THE EIGHTEENTH CENTURY

——— Limit of original Cherokee claims
≡≡≡ Boundary after Revolution

again. Yet the Cherokees have always survived, Phoenix-like, to rebuild.

The Cherokees were said to be a people of fire. Some believed that this was truly their origin. According to ancient legend, they were given an eternal fire. The creator of life, this sacred fire, was the exclusive property of the Cherokee people. When it was once stolen by a conjurer, they sent a young warrior to recover it. Many fullbloods believed that as long as the flame of the sacred fire burned, the Cherokee people would survive. The flame at times smoldered, appearing to be extinguished, but again burst forth with still a brighter blaze. In their beloved Oklahoma hills, the ceremonial fire of the fullblood Cherokee burns brightly today. And the whole Cherokee people believe themselves, like their fire, to be immortal.

Rarely has the flame of the Cherokee burned lower than in the years following the American Revolution. Remaining faithful to their treaties with England, the Cherokees suffered a shattering defeat. The people stood unprotected and unprepared to face an unknown future, the new world the white man had created. "The Death Song of the Cherokees" seemed, at this time, an appropriate air.

Then, just as the Nineteenth Century was dawning, the embers of the eternal fire brightened and the smoldering flame burst forth. The Cherokees embarked on a path which their friends, Washington and Jefferson, had suggested — a complete governmental system based upon the rule of written law. How and why the Cherokees chose this path continually occupies the thoughts of the serious student of Indian history. The reasons were many. The result was singular. With great difficulty the Cherokees laid the groundwork for survival and accomplishment in a world dominated by the new inhabitants of their country.

This transformation from "Intrepid Warriors" to "Civilized Tribe" was not an easy one. Cherokee lifeways were recast and the whole fiber of society was rewoven. Material aspects of tribal life were turned upside down in the course of the struggle to retain the spirit of what was really Cherokee. No historical date can be precisely fixed for this tribal determination to face the white man on his own ground. The decision itself may, nonetheless, have been the most important single event in Cherokee history. Many leading Cherokees deserve credit for these vital and fateful changes. Among this distinguished group are names which ornament Cherokee history — Pathkiller, Hicks, Rogers, Martin, Ridge, Ross, Bushyhead, Foreman, McLemore, Cordery, Starr, Vann, Benge, Fields, Dreadfulwater, Jolly, Lowery, Shorey and Taylor, to name only a few.

To understand the Cherokee people requires a deeper view of the North American Indian. The

10

GEORGE LOWERY, about 1840. Painting attributed to George Catlin, but most probably the work of John Mix Stanley. Lowery held most offices in the tribe but was far more significant as an informal leader. He is credited with securing tribal adoption and support for Sequoyah's syllabary. He wears elaborate early Cherokee silverwork in the nose and ears in traditional fashion. Lowery was one of the last Cherokees thus to stretch the ears in the aboriginal manner. He also is shown wearing a silver nose-plug, massive silver gorget supporting a James Monroe U. S. Presidential Peace Medal, with historic Cherokee wampum belts over each shoulder.

Cherokees are not now, nor have they ever been, horsemen of the plains. They were originally woodland people who had begun the cultivation of the soil long before the arrival of the first European. They had built houses and tended farms for many centuries before they were "proffered civilization." Never at any time did they admit themselves to be "lawless savages." The reports of the earliest explorers and traders support the belief that the Cherokees were among the most advanced of the native North American Indian tribes.

The historic Cherokees were not a nomadic people but lived a rather settled life in permanent villages built along the rivers and streams of the southern mountains. Families lived in wooden houses, doubtless originally built of small limbs, later covered with a clay or mud-like mixture, and then finished off like arbors. Near the center of the village was the septilateral clan house in which religious meetings, social gatherings and councils were held. The sacred fire constantly burned in the center of this edifice. The Cherokee Village, recently built by the revitalized Cherokee Nation near Tahlequah, Oklahoma, is fairly representative of an early tribal town.

The botanist William Bartram noted that the "common plantations" of the tribe surrounded the village. Here the villagers grew crops such as beans, sweet potatoes, corn, tobacco, and squash

12

in the large fields and in the small individual plots. The Cherokee women supplemented the garden foods they cooked with game from the common hunts their men conducted and with fish from the streams, as well as with bountiful wild fruits, vegetables and nuts. Planting, caring for and curing the sacred tobacco was a task of paramount importance to a people like the Cherokees. Tobacco was central to social, religious and healing practices.

Bartram also supplied us with an illuminating description of the Cherokees as they lived at the virtual beginning of the Revolutionary War. "The Cherokees in their disposition and manners are grave and steady, dignified and circumspect in their deportment, yet frank, cheerful and humane; tenacious of the liberties and natural rights of man; secret, deliberate and determined in their councils; honest, just and liberal, and always ready to sacrifice every pleasure and gratification, even their blood and life itself, to defend their territory and maintain their rights."

Warfare and hunting were the traditional occupations of the ancient Cherokee male. Likewise, food planting and gathering, pottery-making, and early child-training were traditional occupations of the Cherokee woman. Children played at learning their adult roles as well as the games and dances of the Cherokees. The child's clan and supervision came from the mother's family in the tribe's matrilineal society, and a

13

boy's mother's brother took primary responsibility for training him to hunt and to fight.

Traditional Cherokee society was organized into seven clans which the eminent Cherokee historian, Dr. Emmet Starr, lists as the Bird, Blind Savannah, Deer, Holly, Long Hair, Paint and Wolf clans. The ancient government had a war-peace dichotomy and organized itself under the renowned Atta-Culla-Culla (The Little Carpenter), Oconostota, and Dragging Canoe into a white (or peace) structure and a red (or war) structure. Their power rested in a Council of the Seven Clans which met at Chota, their ancient capital on the Tennessee River, with the red government ruling in time of war and the white government in time of peace. Life centered around the ceremonial complex with social and political life fixed by the spiritual beliefs. Tribal political unity was a product of historic times, a response to the challenge of colonial invasion.

A series of religious festivals marked the changing of the seasons and the progression of the years. Typical of these ceremonials was the first fruit or green corn which for the Cherokees, like most of their woodland neighbors, celebrated the beginning of a new series of religious activties. The "green corn" was a literal and symbolic religious cleansing at which time this new food was eaten and the old sins and retributions forgiven.

A NEW ORDER

The substitution of a civil state for this religious state constituted a major Cherokee event of the last half of the Eighteenth Century. The survival of the ancient complex could have prevented the internal political, social, and economic changes so important to the emerging Cherokee state. Gradually Cherokee leaders were chosen from those of their number with important connections in Charles Town, Philadelphia, and Washington. The new leadership was a reality by the end of the second decade of the Nineteenth Century. The "New Cherokee State" became a model which the United States hoped other tribes would emulate. Millions of words have been written about this amazing development by writers looking for a romantic people whose noble struggle could inspire the world. Indeed, this is the very vision of current Cherokee leadership. The sacred fire burns brighter day by day.

The Cherokees have always attracted distinguished men to their cause. Among these number Emerson, Thoreau, John Howard Payne, Davy Crocket, Sam Houston, William Wirt, Daniel Webster, Henry Clay, and a whole list of Adamses and Polks. Moreover, they placed on their council table a solid silver pipe from George Washington and always told visitors that the same hand of Thomas Jefferson that had

15

written the Declaration of Independence had also helped them to draft their early laws. The Cherokees took pride in the knowledge that they were a people of respect and of law who understood when and how to use that respect in a lawful process.

The tragedy of the Cherokee people is that too often they have stood divided in so many of their struggles. The Cherokees have been content to entrust their fate to the federal government and to cast themselves into the American mainstream. As one highly educated Cherokee woman, the hundred year old granddaughter of the revered Rev. Stephen Foreman, recently told the press: "Cherokees are American citizens and we have always supported the American flag. Unfortunately, this Cherokee faith has not always been repaid." She could have added that the Cherokee Nation has always striven faithfully to uphold its treaty obligations.

The failure of the United States to respect its treaty commitments is a well-documented story. The Cherokees were told before 1800 that if they would modify their hunter-life and become farmers and merchants and men of property they could retain their ancient homeland forever. The very triumph of the tribe in so quickly transforming itself seems to have encouraged the citizens of Georgia and eventually the President of the United States to seek either their removal or their dissolution as a

16

Cheraquís.

TEXAS CHEROKEES ABOUT 1830. Members of a branch of the Western Cherokees who had migrated to Spanish Texas as early as 1818, they were painted by a Mexican artist near Nacagdoches. There the tribe lived on specific land grants made by Mexico and later solemnly secured by the Republic of Texas. One of the remaining unsettled Cherokee claims grows out of these Texas grants and treaties. Mexican artist Lino Sanchez y Tapia's Cherokee woman appears remarkably Hispanic in hairdo and dress style, causing one to wonder whether the Texas Cherokees adapted rapidly to Spanish-Mexican customs or the artist depicted them more in terms of his own culture than they actually were.

nation. Be it said to the credit of government leaders that the Cherokees could have remained in their eastern homeland by simply accepting state citizenship. A small number did this. Yet the vast unwilling majority was eventually forced to join its brothers west of the Mississippi who had voluntarily gone there under a series of solemn treaties of land exchange negotiated in 1817, 1819, 1828 and 1833. A venturesome few, under The Bowl, departed west as early as 1794 because of a previous untoward event relating to the Cherokee grant of free use of the Tennessee River. The band finally became known as the Texas Cherokees, later to be decimated by the Republic of Texas against the pledged word of its friend, Sam Houston.

By October, 1808, a clear division of thought had broken the tribe into two distinct segments — one desirous of continuing the traditional hunter life, the other committed to the new ways of their white neighbors. The leaders of both sides jointly appealed to their friend President Jefferson, asking his aid in fairly resolving the dilemma. In early January, 1809, this great leader patiently and wisely replied:

> The United States, my children, are the friends of both parties, and as far as can be reasonably asked, they are willing to satisfy the wishes of both. Those who remain may be assured of our patronage, our aid, and good neighborhood...Those who wish to

remove, are permitted [to do so]. . .Every aid toward their removal, and what will be necessary for them there will then be freely administered to them: [after their settlement west of the Mississippi,] we shall still consider them as our children,. . .and always hold them firmly by the hand. Eventually, some 6,000 traditional Cherokees including Sequoyah and Oo-loo-teka, or John Jolly, acted on Jefferson's advice, exchanging their prorata shares of the ancestral domain for an extensive acreage in Arkansas Territory. Later they were known as Old Settlers or Western Cherokees and were eventually removed to an area in present Oklahoma.

The remaining Cherokees dedicated themselves to the new order. The recent restoration of sites in the Cherokee national capitol at New Echota, Georgia, offers proof of the magnitude of their success. There they built a court house, a newspaper office, homes and other buildings. By 1828 the tribe was operating its government under an efficient constitution complete with separation of powers similar to the U. S. system. Federal statistical data indicate that this young nation had, by the third decade of the Nineteenth Century, become a people of substantial properties, at least on a par with their neighbors.

A statement made by the Rev. Samuel A. Worcester most clearly demonstrates the outstanding Cherokee achievement. The vision of Jefferson seemed to have been virtually fulfilled.

19

"The printed constitution and laws of your nation," Worcester wrote to the brilliant young Cherokee scholar, David Brown, "show your progress in civil polity. As far as my knowledge extends, they are executed with a good degree of efficiency, and their execution meets with not the least hindrance from anything like a spirit of insubordination among the people. I do not know of a single family who depend, in any considerable degree, on game for support. The houses of the Cherokees are of all sorts; from an elegant painted or brick mansion, down to a very mean log cabin. If we speak, however, of the mass of the people, they live in comfortable log houses, generally one story high, but frequently two. As to education, the number who can read and write English is considerable, though it bears but a moderate proportion to the whole population. Among such, the degree of improvement and intelligence is various. The Cherokee language, as far as I can judge, is read and written by a large majority of those between childhood and middle age."

The last statement by Worcester refers to the Cherokee syllabary, one of the most remarkable literary accomplishments in the history of mankind. By 1828, Cherokees were reading and writing in their ancient language when only ten years before there had been no syllabary. This outstanding achievement resulted from the work of Sequoyah (Si-kwa-yi), or George Guess, one

SEQUOYAH, OR GEORGE GUESS, 1771-1843, portrayed pointing to one of the characters in the Cherokee syllabary he invented. His costume is that of the traditional Cherokees, and includes the hunting jacket typical of the Western Cherokees. The medal could be the one presented to him by the Cherokee people in honor of his invention of "The Talking Leaves."

of the very few men in the history of the world to invent a syllabary. His creation brought literacy to the Cherokees almost overnight. By 1846, the editor of the *Cherokee Advocate,* William P. Ross, was able to write that "in proportion to population, there are fewer Cherokees who cannot read and write either Cherokee or English, than are found in many states of the union." Millions of pages were published in this Cherokee language. With the aid of the missionaries, the Cherokees brought forth biblical tracts, the *New Testament,* school books and hymnals. They published their own newspapers, *The Cherokee Phoenix,* and later at Tahlequah, *The Cherokee Advocate,* and, in addition, their public laws.

THE CHEROKEE REMOVAL

The Cherokees had been long committed to follow the path of peace. Legend teaches that in the beginning Cherokees were given both the book and the bow but did not use the book and so were left with the bow. The elders say that was why, for a time, the Cherokees appeared to have been overcome. In the lengthy struggle of the 1830's to retain their homes and farms in the "old Country," the Cherokees turned not to the bow but to the book and the law.

To the everlasting credit of the Cherokee people, they stood with honor against the avaricious whites who were determined to drive them from their ancestral homelands. The election of President Jackson in 1828 coincided with the discovery of gold on Cherokee land in Georgia. These two events, coupled with perfected take-over plans and federal commitments in the "Georgia Compact," forced the fatal confrontation. Confiscatory acts and other repressive personal restrictions in the 1830's were Georgia's official rewards to the Indian people who had followed the white man's way. This, despite the fact that President Jefferson had consented to remove the tribes in Georgia only if it could be accomplished "peaceably" and "upon reasonable terms."

The Cherokees were, however, not devoid of white friends. Many good men and women of Georgia stood with them, and were mortified by and deeply resentful of the ill treatment accorded them. Also among this group were many in the Congress who fought the Jackson Removal Bill. Although constantly provoked by border ruffians and intruders, the Cherokees determined to remain peaceful and pursue their legal rights. When Rev. Worcester and other men of God were convicted by Georgia authorities, another Cherokee friend and three-time Attorney General of the United States, William Wirt, took their case to the Supreme Court. For this noble effort, Wirt charged no fee.

As the Cherokees awaited the decision of the court, they determined to obey the law despite

23

its implications. As the eminent and classically educated Elias Boudinot observed perceptively in *The Cherokee Phoenix:* "The Cherokees are for justice and they are trying to obtain it in a peaceable manner by a regular course of law. If the last and legitimate tribunal decides against them, as honest men the Cherokees will submit and 'the agony will be over.' Will Georgia be as honest and submit to her own [United States] courts?"

The Supreme Court rendered its decision in 1832. In an opinion written by Chief Justice John Marshall, the court held: "The Cherokee Nation is a distinct community, occupying its own territory, with boundaries accurately described, in which, the citizens of Georgia have no right to enter but with the assent of the Cherokees themselves or in conformity with treaties and with the acts of Congress. The whole intercourse between the United States and this nation is, by our Constitution and laws, vested in the government of the United States."

The Supreme Court supported the Cherokee cause, but Georgia turned away from the book and took up the bow, as did the President. Andrew Jackson reputedly stated: "John Marshall has made his law, now let him enforce it." The court had no soldiers, but Jackson did. While the Reverend Worcester languished in prison at Milledgeville, Georgia, the Cherokee removal controversy heightened to the breaking

24

ELIAS BOUDINOT, 1802-1839. See page 84 for biography.

ELIAS CORNELIUS BOUDINOT, 1835-1890, son of Elias.

ELIAS C. BOUDINOT II, 1854-1896, Cherokee attorney; Elias's grandson; Elias C.'s nephew.

FRANK J. BOUDINOT, 1866-1945; Cherokee attorney; Elias C. II's brother.

point. The tribe led by Principal Chief John Ross remained quiet, however, retaining its faith in the sanctity of the law.

Yet a proper course of Cherokee conduct was difficult in the face of the President's attitude toward removal. Tribal leaders, many of whom had fought under General Jackson in the War of 1812, had split into two determined factions. Major Ridge and his compatriots argued that emigration was inevitable. They contended that the tribe should work to arrange the best and safest removal to the region beyond the Mississippi. Chief Ross, however, wished to resist the clearly illegal removal, hoping that congressional and religious pressures and probably a change in the national administration would prevent it. Nevertheless, the Ridge faction executed a treaty at New Echota in December, 1835, the signers of which, including Andrew Ross, the chief's brother, and their supporters became known as the "Treaty Party." John Ross, leading the great majority of the Cherokees, denounced the accord and utterly refused to prepare for the removal despite the constant clamor of intruders infiltrating Cherokee country.

Eventually, in 1837-38 the United States sent troops to remove the people forcibly. The tragic task of gathering the Cherokees, including the sick, the lame, the blind, and especially the children, and forcing them to the West fell upon

JOHN ROSS, 1790-1866, Principal Chief. The life of John Ross was the personification of the life of the Cherokee Nation. See page 83 for biography.

Major General Winfield Scott. The general's autobiography sheds light upon the depth of his feeling in carrying out the gravest mission of his entire military career: "Food in abundance had been provided at the depots, and wagons accompanied every detachment of troops. Before the first night thousands – men, women, and children, sick and well – were brought in. Poor creatures. They had obstinately refused to prepare for the removal. Many arrived half starved, but refused the food that was pressed upon them. At length, the children, with less pride, gave way, and next their parents. The Georgians were the waiters on the occasion, many of them with flowing tears. The autobiographer has never witnessed a scene of deeper pathos." Yet, in the end, 15,000 Cherokees were driven by force of arms from their beloved southern mountains. Only 11,000, it is said, finished the journey which came to be known as "The Trail of Tears."

A NEW NATION IN THE WEST

A people of less determination might have been destroyed by the tragedy of removal. The internal strife created by the pre-removal controversy was almost fatal. In June, 1839, shortly after the arrival of the Ross Cherokees in Indian Territory, the brilliant leadership of the Treaty Party was emasculated by the brutal and bloody assassinations of Major Ridge, John Ridge, Elias

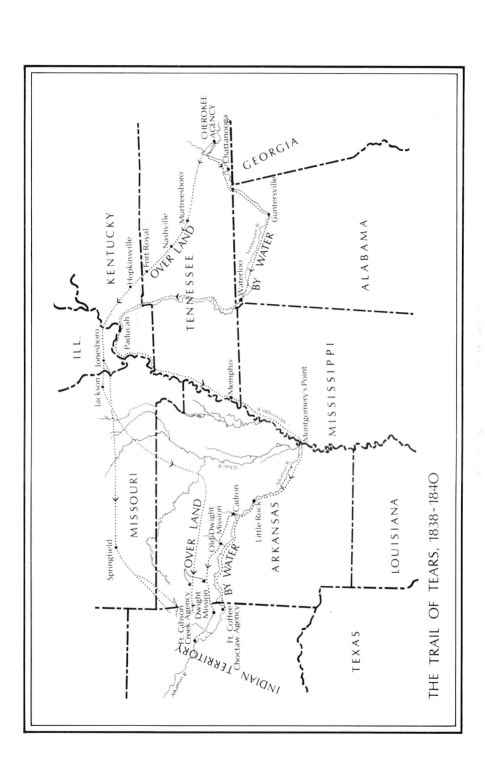

THE TRAIL OF TEARS, 1838–1840

MAJOR RIDGE, 1771-1839, one of the most significant, if not the most significant, figure of Cherokee adaptation of customs and standards from the whites. See page 86.

Boudinot, and James Starr, among others. This event cast a shadow over the political union of the Eastern-Emigrant or Ross Party members and the Western or Old Settler Cherokees as envisioned by a new Cherokee constitution adopted in September, 1839. Moreover, it precipitated a near-suicidal intra-tribal war that lasted until 1846.

Following the Treaty of 1846, which partially settled many grave intra-tribal disputes, the tribe entered into what has often been called "The Golden Age of the Cherokee." During this time the nation consolidated its extraordinary advances begun in Georgia. The Cherokees revived a tribal newspaper, *The Cherokee Advocate,* books, pamphlets, and broadsides. Even more amazing was the progress made in education and government. Notwithstanding the tragedy of removal and the reduction of their country to ashes by the Civil War, they established a college and 126 public schools, graduating men and women of talent and competency. No wonder that Cherokees have provided leadership in every vocation and calling and have added immeasurably to the educational, socio-economic, and cultural development of the state in which they now reside!

In the years following removal, Park Hill became the cultural and intellectual center of the little nation. Rose Cottage, the home of Chief John Ross, was the center of Park Hill. An early observer described the plantation and the life of the family which lived there: "Situated on high ground overlooking a wide sweep of country, the white house, surrounded by a fence covered with rose vines, must have surprised and delighted guests. The cottage could hold forty guests in comfort. Here, the Ross family lived in great style, and kept open house."

One often hears that the prosperity of the Cherokees in the 1850's stopped with the well-to-do mixed bloods. The stately antebellum home, the Murrell House, in "Old" Park Hill, it is said, reflected the elegant lifestyle of only a few. Yet, John Ross, only one-eighth Cherokee by blood, was the most popular chief among the fullbloods, who themselves enjoyed a standard of living as high as, if not better than, their neighbors in Arkansas, Kansas, or Missouri. Their educational system was undoubtedly superior. Thus, without any aid from the United States, the Cherokees built a nation which was described by many as the "Athens of the West."

The Cherokee census records list land use, cattle, and other property of all tribal members. The nation's land resources were available to all its citizens, and poverty was practically unknown. Economic opportunity was open to all, and the fruits thereof abounded in such measure that the so-called wealth of individual families was not at the expense of their fellow Cherokees. The Rev. Samuel Worcester himself noted:

REVEREND SAMUEL A. WORCESTER, 1798-1859.

"But, it will be asked, is the improvement which has been described, general among the people, and are the fullblooded Indians civilized, or only the half-bloods? I answer that, in the description which I have given, I have spoken of the mass of the people, without distinction. If it be asked, however, what class are most advanced – I answer, as a general thing – those of mixed blood...But, though those of mixed blood are generally in the van, yet the whole mass of the people is on the march."

In Indian Territory, the Cherokee future was cast by geographic location. Hence, the Cherokees found it impossible to avoid becoming enbroiled in the Civil War. At the outbreak of hostilities, protective federal troops were needed elsewhere, leaving the Cherokees surrounded by southern armies. Chief Ross' policy of neutrality was intolerable to those leaders sympathetic to the South, and the tribe in late 1861 broke over and entered the conflict.

Little purpose would be served here by retracing the course of the war in the Cherokee Nation. The tribe was almost equally divided, and the country ultimately devastated. From neutrality, the nation under extreme duress initially embraced an allegiance with the South. Finally, Chief Ross, insisting that he had been coerced into the Confederacy, went north in 1862 and there consulted with Abraham Lincoln and his cabinet until the war's end. Meanwhile, the conflict continued in Indian Territory — Cherokee against Cherokee. Most of the Cherokee Nation went up in flames. The brave Cherokee general, Stand Watie, held out to become the last Confederate general to surrender. As the war ended, the Cherokee Nation, like the Shenandoah Valley in Virginia, was truly a desolate, burnt-over land.

Notwithstanding the fealty of Chief Ross and the loyalty of over 2,200 Cherokee soldiers who had gallantly served the Union, the United States Interior Department adopted a hostile attitude toward the tribe upon termination of hostilities. This posture developed even before the assassination of President Lincoln and continued through the administration of President Andrew Johnson. By punishing the whole Cherokee people, the government hoped to strip the nation of a vast portion of its fee title property acquired in exchange for the Cherokee country east of the Mississippi River and in Arkansas.

In September, 1865, five federal commissioners, including a high ranking army officer, convened at Fort Smith, Arkansas, to negotiate "new treaties" with the Five Civilized Tribes. Peculiarly, their attention focused on Principal Chief John Ross, whom they hoped to divest of tribal leadership. The official minutes of the private meetings of the commissioners contain a communication from Secretary of the Interior

James Harlan, a former United States senator from Iowa, which endorsed the plan:

> I am satisfied in view of the facts and circumstances in the case that it would be for the benefit of the great Cherokee Nation that their present Chief John Ross be deposed from his said office of Principal Chief of the Cherokee Nation.

Harlan's directive to oust the venerable leader in effect falsely charged the loyal Union Cherokees and the southern battalions led by Stand Watie with treason. He followed this decision with an even more pre-emptory one:

> Your telegram of 16th in relation to John Ross has been submitted to the President. He authorizes and directs me to say that on your understanding of the facts as stated, your action is approved.
>
> Should he persist you are authorized to recognize such other party or parties as representative of the Cherokee Nation, as may appear to you to be the true representatives of their sentiments and wishes. And should those who have been in rebellion against the Government of the United States refuse to harmonize with the loyal portion of the Nation, you will recognize as the organ of each party such persons as seem to you to be the true representatives of their sentiments and wishes. . . .

At the next regular meeting of the commissioners, Chairman D. N. Cooley officially deposed John Ross. The great chief was present

36

CONFEDERATE BRIGADIER GENERAL STAND WATIE, 1806-1871, brother of Elias Boudinot and last southern general to surrender at the end of the Civil War. See page 85.

and although extremely humiliated and mortified, he inquired if he could make "a few remarks." The chairman permitting, the articulate Ross extemporaneously responded:

"Sir, I deny the charges asserted against me. I deny having used any influence, either with the Cherokees, Creeks, or any other persons to resist the interests of the Indians, or of the Gov. of the U. S. I came to this place, Sir, at the special invitation and urgent request that I should do so. . . .I defy any person to come forward and prove these charges against me, who will state the truth.

"I know prejudices have existed against me for years past, but, Sir, I have maintained a peaceful course throughout my whole life. I claim to be as loyal a man as any other citizen of the U. S. There are certain documents which have found their way upon your table and which I signed. I have testimony which I hope I may be permitted to lay before you on that subject. I have been forty odd years Chief of the Cherokees, elected time after time. They reelected me in my absence and I came on at my advanced age, after burying my wife and burying my son. I had three sons in your army, also three grandsons and three nephews. If I had been disloyal I would not have shrunk from going in the direction where the enemies of the U. S. were. . . .

If we have rights, we ought to be permitted to express them. I never recommended any other course than that which could be sustained consistent with the laws of the U. S. I have been three years residing in Washington. I have been in communication with the Department, Sir, with the President. With Mr. Lincoln I was constantly in communication, and up to the last moment I communicated with the present President U. S.

I have never been charged with being an enemy of the U. S. I hope I may be permitted to make a respectful statement in reply to what has been preferred against me. . . ."

Clearly, the commissioners hoped to shake the confidence of the Cherokee leaders in their reliance upon former treaties by threats of forfeiture of property and accusations of treason. The adamant position of Chief Ross, of H. D. Reece, and of other prominent Cherokees, many of whom had fought with valor in Union ranks, made the attempt a failure. Ground work had, however, been laid by the commissioners to set the scene for woes yet to come the following year in Washington.

In the capital city in the spring and summer of 1866 lengthy negotiations proceeded with two Cherokee delegations, Union and Confederate, vying for official recognition. Chief Ross was not permitted to be heard personally in any of the negotiations. He died on August 1 after lingering for weeks in his room in a hotel in

Washington. Meanwhile, Union-Cherokee delegates agreed to a treaty on July 19. Evidence that the government had second thoughts about excluding Ross is reflected by the "title" to the Treaty of 1866 which states that the dying "Principal Chief of the Cherokee Nation was too unwell to join in these negotiations." One can only conjecture that this tardy respect even so faintly rendered resulted from an effort to conciliate the Union-Cherokee delegates and hasten the end of the proceedings. The chief's remains were temporarily interred on the banks of the Brandywine near Wilmington, Delaware, later to be re-interred "in the cemetery near his once lovely home at Park Hill, five miles from Tahlequah."

A MATURE POLITICAL STATE

The Civil War marked the end of a formative era in Cherokee history. The tribe and its people emerged as a mature political state. The title "Cherokee Nation" given in the Treaty of 1791 and proclaimed by President Washington was especially appropriate for the people at this time. Indeed, if ever a North American aboriginal group stood ready to assume the responsibilities of statehood, the Cherokees of the 1867 to 1900 era were such a people. Mature political and social institutions had emerged; public offices had established continuity; their educational seminaries were reopened; the sound

CONFEDERATE CHEROKEE DELEGATES to Washington in 1866. (Left to right) John Rollin Ridge, grandson of Major Ridge; Saladin Watie, son of Brigadier General Stand Watie; Judge Richard Fields; Elias Cornelius Boudinot; and William Penn Adair. Kinship played a fundamental role in Cherokee national politics. General Stand Watie occupied a key place in the Ridge-Watie-Boudinot leadership. Major Ridge was his uncle; John Ridge was a cousin; John Rollin Ridge was a nephew. Stand Watie's brother, Elias Boudinot, took the name of a New England benefactor. Together, this group was influential in urging removal of the Cherokees from the East and signing the Treaty of New Echota in an effort to prevent the tragedy that became known as the "Trail of Tears." Watie narrowly escaped the 1839 political assassinations.

farming and merchant economy extended into all levels of Cherokee society; the nation was prosperous and capable of educating its children, protecting its orphans, and punishing its criminals, at no cost whatever to the federal government.

The not wholly unexpected result of removal had been to create three powerful divisions within the nation, whose problems from then until now have engaged the attention of government officials. The Eastern or Emigrant Cherokees, the Western or Old Settler Cherokees, and the Treaty Party comprise these three large components of the tribe. Furthermore, there exist eight other important intra-tribal business, social and religious bands whose rituals, traditions, affairs and leaders are generally known and respected by everyone well acquainted with the Cherokee people. These bands, together with the approximate dates of their respective origins, are as follows:

The Seven Clan Society . . . . Ancient
The Four Mothers' Society, with
    some fullblood Creek members . Ancient
The Texas Cherokees 1819
The Keetoowah Society 1856
The Nighthawk Keetoowahs 1861
The Delaware Cherokees 1867
The Shawnee Cherokees 1868
The United Keetoowah Band, a
    federally chartered corporation . . .1950

Two of these bands are the descendants of those Delawares and Shawnees who purchased property rights in the Cherokee Nation by the Treaty of 1866. All of these bands are known to the government and together with the three federally recognized divisions aggregate more than 35,000. Together with their descendants, they are commonly known as members or citizens of the Cherokee Nation by blood. They actually constitute the tribe today. Considerable overlapping of membership within these bands is generally well known.

DISSOLUTION OF
TRIBAL GOVERNMENT

Pursuant to a series of federal statutes ending in the early 1900's, the Commission to the Five Civilized Tribes, also known as the Dawes Commission, took over the Cherokee government. By action of this commission, two groups of non-Indians known as "political citizens" were listed on separate tribal rolls. One group, the intermarried whites, was permitted citizenship rights by custom of the nation prior to 1875. In 1906, the U. S. Supreme Court held that all intermarried whites who had married a Cherokee citizen by blood prior to 1875 were entitled to be enrolled as citizens of the nation for all purposes; and white persons marrying subsequent to 1875 were by the decision in this case deprived of such rights.

The other group, called Freedmen, became political citizens of the Cherokee Nation under terms of the Treaty of 1866 and those of the amended Cherokee Constitution of the same year. The Freedmen were ex-slaves formerly owned by individual Cherokees, and free blacks lawfully residing within the tribal domain in 1861 and their descendants. The Cherokee Nation itself did not own any slaves. In fact, in February of 1863, prior to President Lincoln's Emancipation Proclamation, the tribe had emancipated all slaves within its domain. These particular rolls were prepared by the Dawes Commission, and federal law allowed these non-Indian citizens equal interest and participation in the distribution of Cherokee tribal property, including land and money. Oklahoma and all other states would confront the same situation if, today, their public lands and buildings were ordered sold by a higher power and the money distributed per capita among *all* the citizens of such states.

As established by the Dawes Commission, the original final rolls of *all* political citizens of the Cherokee national government contained in the aggregate 41,889 citizens, including full and lesser degrees of Cherokee blood, adopted Delawares and Shawnees, and Intermarried Whites and Freedmen. Congress further directed that allotments of lands in severalty from the nation's fee title domain to the political citizens

Courtesy Thomas Gilcrease Institute

TRADITIONAL CHEROKEE KEE-TOO-WAHS participating in a religious ceremony around the sacred fire about 1930. At the Redbird Smith Grounds, a group of Cherokees celebrates the feeding of the fire with the blood of a white chicken. The logs surrounding the fire are pointed in the four cardinal directions, and the fire is made from seven types of wood. The sacred fire has been kindled on a small earthen mound reminiscent of the much larger ceremonial mounds of earlier times. A stickball pole topped by a wooden fish can be seen in the background.

of the Cherokee Nation be based upon these federal rolls.

THE REVITALIZED
CHEROKEE NATION

The final congressional act in the series designed to end the Cherokee government and to pave the way for Oklahoma statehood, for reasons then best known to Congress, made an important distinction between the Cherokee tribe and the Cherokee tribal government. The measure continued indefinitely both institutions as they now exist in Oklahoma using the following words:

SEC. 28. The Tribal existence and present Tribal governments of the Choctaw, Chickasaw, Cherokee, Creek and Seminole Tribes or Nations are hereby continued in full force and effect for all purposes authorized by law, until otherwise provided by law.

This provision of federal law, except in respect to the Choctaw Nation, has remained unchanged from the date of its enactment. Under its authority the Cherokees through the years, by direction of special jurisdictional acts, have been allowed to litigate some of their legal and moral claims against the people and government of the United States.

In 1961, one of the Cherokees' most noted cases resulted in a judgement in favor of the

46

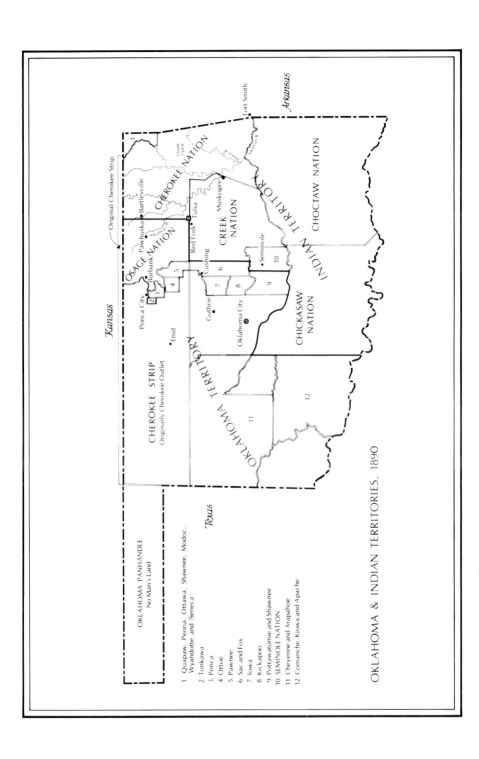

OKLAHOMA & INDIAN TERRITORIES, 1890

OKLAHOMA PANHANDLE
No Man's Land

1. Quapaw, Peoria, Ottawa, Shawnee, Modoc,
   Wyandotte and Seneca
2. Tonkawa
3. Ponca
4. Ottoe
5. Pawnee
6. Sac and Fox
7. Iowa
8. Kickapoo
9. Pottawatomie and Shawnee
10. SEMINOLE NATION
11. Cheyenne and Arapahoe
12. Comanche, Kiowa and Apache

CHEROKEE STRIP
Originally Cherokee Outlet

Original Cherokee Strip

Kansas

Texas

Arkansas

OSAGE NATION

CHEROKEE NATION

CREEK NATION

CHOCTAW NATION

CHICKASAW NATION

OKLAHOMA TERRITORY

INDIAN TERRITORY

Fort Smith
Bartlesville
Pawhuska
Burbank
Ponca City
Enid
Red Fork
Tulsa
Muskogee
Cushing
Seminole
Guthrie
Oklahoma City

Cherokees for the sum of $14,789,000 after lengthy research and ten years of strictly legal effort before the Indian Claims Commission in Washington. The Commission held that in 1893 the Cherokees, against their will and for an unconscionable consideration, had been forced to deed to the government 6,022,000 acres of their fee title land, known as the "Cherokee Outlet" in northwest Oklahoma. This land was the object of the famed Oklahoma Run in September, 1893. In that run, 40,000 U. S. citizens were given free homesteads of 160 acres each, while later in 1902, the 41,000 citizens of the Cherokee Nation were allotted the remainder of their fee domain. Unlike the white settlers, the Cherokee people received only 110 acres each, including the Flint Hills where many fullbloods lived then and remain now. The late Attorney General Robert F. Kennedy wisely and humanely decided not to appeal the decision in the Outlet case. Thereafter, Congress promptly paid the judgement and directed the U. S. Treasury to set up an account on its books for the Cherokee Nation.

In 1962, Congress directed per capita payments to be made from this judgement fund to all persons, or their legal heirs, whose names appeared upon the rolls prepared by the Dawes Commission and finalized by statute on March 4, 1907. The Bureau of Indian Affairs under the direction of the Secretary of the Interior was

48

entrusted with this duty. The detailed work was promptly and efficiently concluded by the Area Director's Office at Muskogee at the Cherokee Nation's expense. More than 80,000 individuals received benefits from this judgement.

The Distribution Act of 1962 also provided that any funds not allocated per capita should revert to the nation and be "advanced and expended" by the Principal Chief and approved by the Secretary of the Interior. At the moment, Principal Chief W. W. Keeler with cabinet members Louella Coon; Neil Morton; J. D. Johnson, Deputy Chief; B. Bob Stopp, Executive Business Director; and Earl Boyd Pierce; Vice-Chiefs Bruce Townsend, Rev. Sam Hider, Richard Chuculate, and Robert W. Swimmer, and the nation's office staff are using the reverted funds to achieve a number of vital objectives. Supporting the work of these officers are an astute Tribal Attorney, Mr. Ross Swimmer; a well qualified Farm Manager, Mr. Dan Hayes; a Housing Commission headed by a fullblood, Mr. Johnny Chopper; an expert Director of Housing activity, Mr. Thomas Mack Crossland; and a trained fullblood specialist in public health, Mrs. Louella Coon. All are engaged in a serious effort to rehabilitate the less fortunate members of the nation, an objective made possible through use of Cherokee funds and substantial assistance from the local, state and federal governments. Nonetheless, many discerning citizens at home and throughout America have asked: "Is the effort too late?" Accomplishments of the revitalization program in recent years demonstrate that it is not. What, then, in concrete terms has been achieved? The statistics show that the Cherokees are truly entering a "Golden Age" of economic and social development. As evidence, many positive factors may be cited.

Employment Opportunities. The prideful Tsa-La-Gi Cultural Center gives seasonal jobs to some 150 people each year, of whom eighty per cent are Cherokees. During the past seven years, total salaries of almost one million dollars have been paid. The Neighborhood Youth Corps program directed by Guy D. Osburn and Don Ade has provided jobs for more than 3,000 young Cherokees. The beautiful Cherokee Restaurant near Tahlequah offers thirty-six full or part-time jobs to Cherokees. The Tahlequah and Catoosa Arts and Crafts centers provide jobs for 150 Cherokee home craftsmen. Four full and two part-time positions are provided year round for Cherokees at these centers with three additional positions during the summer.

Cherokee Nation Industries has had phenomenal growth and success. This company employs approximately 180 Cherokees with a weekly payroll of more than $14,000 and an annual payroll in excess of $800,000. The company operates in the electronic subcontracting field

50

and has sustained fine contractual relations with Western Electric, IBM, American Airlines and other nationally known corporations. Annual sales of Cherokee products from this industry average $2,000,000. The initial investment of the nation amounted to only $20,000, which sum has long since been returned to the treasury.

The Cherokee Nation has investments in the Glassmaster Plastics Company at Grove, Oklahoma, and Stephens Manufacturing Company at Muskogee, Oklahoma, where several Cherokees have found employment. The loan to the latter company was fully repaid in July, 1973. Other Oklahoma companies employ several hundred more citizens of the Cherokee Nation. These include Gould, Inc., at Pryor, where fifty-three of the first seventy-three employees were Indians. Fabric-Cut of Pryor employs 100 Indians in a work force of 145. In the Wagoner, Oklahoma, area, ELTRA will employ 500 persons, and it is believed that more than 100 of the employees will be Cherokees from the Hulbert and Lost City areas. Fourteen other employment projects are within the Cherokee area and presently employ a total of 903 people, 550 of whom are Indians as classified and defined by the Bureau of Indian Affairs and the U. S. Census Bureau.

The Cherokee Nation's land-use programs are well under way with fine management, and soon will be effectively utilized through fullblood enterprise. Approximately 20,000 acres, now in use and worth well over $5,000,000, have been bought and fully paid for under Chief Keeler's administration. This is a remarkable achievement given the fact that the allotment process had stripped the nation of its total land resources, excepting only one river bed. Moreover, the Cherokee Nation's treasury was absolutely depleted in 1916.

Housing and Construction. Programs to meet housing needs are far advanced with nearly 1,200 homes completed and more to come. All mutual help homes and low rent houses are under tribal management. The tribe has also constructed its own office and one occupied by the Bureau of Indian Affairs. Space in these buildings brings an annual rental of nearly $68,000.

In 1967, at the beginning of industrial development, the Cherokee Restaurant and Cherokee Arts and Crafts building were built largely by fullbloods. The Bureau of Indian Affairs under the direction of Virgil N. Harrington, then Area Director, prepared the initial plans for the industrial complex and supervised this first important construction effort. Mr. Harrington's staff of experts, including Abe Lincoln, head of Plant Management, and other faithful government employees provided the fullest cooperation to Chief Keeler and his associates.

52

The tribal office has also established a corporation to engage in contracting and building operations. The Cherokee Nation Builders headed by Jerry Thompson, a young fullblood, employs thirty Cherokees and is engaged in home improvement construction, installation of electrical facilities in low rent housing units, building sewer treatment plants, laying sewer lines, hauling gravel, and laying block and brick. The corporation was one of the first created by any U. S. Indian tribe to become developer and contractor for self-help housing. As of June, 1973, the total contracts of 306 homes awarded to the organization amounted to $3,653,000.

An Indian Action Team has been organized under a non-profit organization known as the Cherokee Nation Construction Company. Capable of receiving grants from the federal government, in 1972 it budgeted $933,655 to provide training in the field of construction for eighty-four students. The company was instrumental in writing proposals for the Osage tribe for $36,000 and the Chickasaw tribe for $210,000, the funding for which is now being utilized for the purposes intended.

Finally, the Cherokee Nation contemplates and has drafted other long range construction plans. These include a supermarket, a poultry processing plant, a nursery, a motel, a marina, a summer youth camp, a hunting lodge, a tomato hot house and an archives building.

53

Educational and Cultural Activities. In the late 1960's, the Cherokee Cultural Center, known as Tsa-La-Gi, was launched under the capable direction of Col. Martin A. Hagerstrand. It has brought thousands of visitors to eastern Oklahoma, providing an economic increment in excess of $20,000,000. The Cherokee Pageant, "The Trail of Tears," now has its own air-conditioned outdoor amphitheater. The play is based on the script prepared by the renowned Dr. Kermit Hunter of Southern Methodist University, who wrote the earlier companion script "Unto These Hills" performed in Cherokee, North Carolina. The thrilling Cherokee music of both pageants was prepared by the late Cherokee composer, Dr. Jack Kilpatrick. "Trail of Tears" as an outdoors pageant has every prospect of becoming as popular and as successful as the famed "Unto These Hills."

The amphitheater, an adjacent replica of a Cherokee village as of about 1700, and the new Cherokee Hall of Fame have been developed under Chief Keeler and Col. Hagerstrand as important components of a comprehensive cultural center which will also include a Cherokee National Museum under construction in 1973, and a Cherokee National Shrine and Library. The detailed plans of all components were prepared by one of the Cherokee Nation's finest young architects, Charles Chief Boyd of Tulsa. Many visitors to the area from outside

54

LEE WILEY (Mrs. Nat Tischenkel), radio and television singing star.

LYNN RIGGS, author and poet, upon whose *Green Grow the Lilacs* the play *Oklahoma* is based.

WILLARD STONE, contemporary sculptor, with some of his work.

Courtesy Muskogee Daily Phoenix

JOAN HILL, winner of every major award for Indian painting, at work.

Oklahoma have been profuse in their praise of both the cultural center and industrial complex. Moreover, virtually every member of the tribe concedes that the revitalization program would have been an outstanding success had nothing more been accomplished than the production and display of this grand evidence of Cherokee accomplishment.

The revitalization program has also been responsible for the establishment of a new Cherokee newspaper, *The Cherokee Nation News,* with subscribers in all parts of the world. This is the third effort of the nation to publish a newspaper. Like the first, *The Cherokee Phoenix* in Georgia, it is managed by Cherokee editors, fullbloods Sue Thompson and Minnie Johnson.

The several communities in the Cherokee country have established a method of disseminating information of tribal activities through an organization known as the Elected Community Representatives. First Hiner Doublehead and later Rev. Sam Hider, both fullblood Cherokees, headed this organization. Its work is most vital to the successful operation of the varied programs inaugurated by Chief Keeler. It has proven effective, furthermore, in encouraging fullblood participation in Cherokee affairs.

The Cherokee Foundation headed by Joyce Hifler Zoffness is a non-profit organization to assist Cherokees. It is supported by private funds. Its basic purpose is to improve the welfare, culture, health and morale of the Cherokee people. It helps young Cherokees obtain higher education through scholarships and loans, or to learn self-supporting trades. It assists in preserving the history of the Cherokee people. In this latter task, it has the admirable support of the Cherokee National Historical Society. As of 1972, the Foundation had spent in excess of $447,000 to carry out its programs and activities.

Social Welfare. As a part of this over-all development, the Bureau of Indian Affairs has carried forward a Home Improvement Program serving fifty-eight Cherokee families with an expenditure of $169,000 in 1972. The Public Health Service has provided more than $1,000,000 in inaugurating and constructing sanitation facilities for individual homes. Hundreds of water wells have been drilled, and practically all of these homes are now modern in every respect.

The Cherokee Nation also sustains a very capable community development program. Its officers are Hiner Doublehead and Johnson O'Field, both fullblood Cherokees of wide respect and acquaintance. Their valuable assistance to fullblood families in eastern Oklahoma has aided greatly in elevating living conditions, increasing employment, providing health care, and encouraging education.

The tribe sponsors a comprehensive sanitation program. Its objective is to coordinate various efforts and to improve the flow of information to the Public Health Service, the Cherokee Nation, the BIA and the Indian people. Earl Crawford of Tahlequah and Johnny Chopper of Jay have long been employed in and dedicated to this effort.

The Cherokee Nation is, furthermore, engaged in a Tribal Assistance Program with a substantial budget supplied by the federal government. More than $500,000 is allocated to cover the various training programs which are managed by seven Cherokee staff members. In 1973, supervision was provided for 264 adult vocational trainees, 114 direct applicants, and 130 on-the-job training participants. Along with this manpower program, the tribe supervises a Work Experience Program with three Cherokee staff members aiding seventy-five participants in learning and preparing to support themselves. The 1972 budget for this program amounted to $190,000, providing a livelihood for some 400 individuals. The tribe also has long supported and operated a clothing outlet for needy Cherokees benefitting a total of 5,586 persons in 1972 alone.

The Tribal Credit Program, headed by half-blood Cherokee Johnny Masters of Jay, was established in 1966 and is monitored by the Bureau of Indian Affairs. The program has completed 101 loans totaling $512,900 from tribal funds. These loans are geared to help worthy Cherokees in need of credit which is otherwise unavailable to them. Mental health programs including a guidance center on alcoholism are also administered by the tribe. Cherokee staff members as well as four counselors work directly with the people for whom such programs are designed.

Eleven specialists work in the Community Health Program headed by Louella Coon. The main objective of this project is to raise the health status of the Indian people through communication and understanding. In thirteen field clinics, two Cherokees counsel with patients on family planning and birth control. In addition, five Cherokee staff members are engaged in identifying, recruiting, motivating, and guiding Indian students of eastern Oklahoma to agencies that will train professional medical personnel for the area.

Finally, an active Boy Scout program is administered by a paraprofessional who works with interested boys of Indian heritage. The program is new but five troops have been organized with eighty-five boy scouts and eleven cub scouts participating in 1973.

Relations with the United States. Spurring the remarkable and noteworthy efforts of self-help housing, improved sanitation and health facilities, employment and educational opportunities, and a creditable industrial complex and cultural center is the animated hope that

Cherokee-federal government affairs arising from treaty obligations will be speedily ended.

In the 1860's and again in the 1890's, Cherokee leaders were almost totally preoccupied with resistance to governmental efforts to reduce the nation's land resources. In the 20th Century, Principal Chiefs Milam and Keeler have striven in the Congress and in the courts to regain a portion of the tribe's lost heritage. For years the Cherokees have found sound reason to distinguish between the untoward acts of individual federal officials and clearly authorized federal policy. Harmful individual acts, for reasons oftentimes obscure, have been difficult to remedy, while both the Congress and the courts have, when appealed to, usually responded with a fair measure of justice.

In this connection, the language of Judge Charles Nott of the Court of Claims in the 1891 Western Cherokee case bears consideration. "The Treaty of New Echota," he said, "was the act and deed of neither the Eastern nor Western Cherokees." This language apparently strikes down the important Treaty of 1835 which necessitated resettlement of the tribe in present Oklahoma, even though this treaty has been enforced by the U. S. from the date of its proclamation. In fact, it was upheld as late as April, 1970, by the United States Supreme Court. Happily, in this latest opinion, the treaty and the patent issued pursuant to its provisions

60

were held to sustain tribal fee title to 100 miles of the valuable and navigable Arkansas River bed in Oklahoma.

Inasmuch as the Court of Claims expressly held in 1891 that neither the Eastern nor Western Cherokees made this 1835 treaty, who, then, was responsible for it? Acting for but hardly in the moral interest of the United States was the notorious J. F. Schermerhorn. For the Cherokee Nation, some twenty prominent and highly trustworthy individuals assembled to represent it. Yet as Chief Ross stated, these Cherokees possessed no legal authority to bind the nation and its people to the terms of the treaty. They were not chiefs nor headmen *elected* to treat away the dearest possessions of the nation, nor were they delegated to act by either the national council or the Principal Chief. The Treaty of 1835 was, therefore, the work of agents of the United States who failed to recognize the constituted authorities of the Cherokee people. No wonder, then, that Judge Nott's truthful but specific language has never been modified!

The 1835 accord was, of course, a treaty of cession and not of amity, whereas the subsequent Treaty of 1846 was an agreement of amity and, importantly, of mutual intra-tribal concessions. Yet the latter treaty relieved the United States of liability for depriving the Western Cherokees of exclusive title to the equivalent of 8,000,000 acres of land, or two-thirds of their holdings, by confirming title to the entire Cherokee acreage in Oklahoma to the nation as a whole. In 1828, the Western Cherokees had acquired full title to all Cherokee land in Oklahoma, yet in 1835 the United States conveyed that same land to the Eastern Cherokees.

Another example of how individuals representing the government have dealt curiously with the Cherokee people comes from the work of the so-called Jerome Commission in 1891. In order to induce the tribe to sell the Cherokee Outlet in northwestern Oklahoma, the commission solemnly *promised* to render an accounting for all expenditures of Cherokee trust funds from 1787, in addition to agreeing to pay $8,595,000 for the tract (or $1.29 per acre). The commission simultaneously refused, however, to account for the true Cherokee land acreage purchased, granted, and secured to them by government patent in 1838. The commission assured the Cherokees in writing, on the other hand, that if an official accounting of tribal funds expended from the federal treasury resulted in a balance due the Cherokees, it would be forthwith paid by the Congress if then in session and by the next ensuing Congress if not.

The Cherokee Outlet agreement of 1891 including the written promises which constituted a vital part of the consideration for the sale was duly ratified and approved by the President on March 3, 1893. On that date, the United States assumed that it had lawfully acquired the title to and in part took possession of the celebrated Cherokee Outlet. In September of that year, 6,022,000 acres of it were homesteaded free by 40,000 citizens of the United States with 160 acres to each one. The remaining portion of the Outlet, some 2,121,978 acres, was assigned by Congressional acts to six other "friendly" Indian Tribes including the Osage, Kaws, Pawnees, Poncas, Otoes and Tonkawas.

Yet the story has had a happy if belated ending. Thanks to the courts, these costly and unfortunate individual acts were not permitted to stand. Sixty-eight years after the event, in 1961, the U. S. Indian Claims Commission first held after a lengthy and expensive law suit, that the entire Outlet had been obtained by duress and for an unconscionable consideration. Eventually in a 1961 and a 1973 decision, the Commission awarded judgements to the Cherokee Nation aggregating nearly $19,000,000 without interest, as additional payment for the land.

It is not only pertinent but it is completely just to note that many individuals produced these astounding results for the Cherokee people. These included the late Principal Chief J.

Bartley Milam; Principal Chief W. W. Keeler; the original Cherokee Executive Committee and its ever faithful and efficient executive secretary Marie L. Wadley; and the patient and skilled attorney, Paul M. Niebell.

The brilliant son of a Baptist minister, Mr. Niebell is not a Cherokee. Through all the years of the actual litigation, he cautioned his associate attorneys to be fully mindful of the historic importance of the Outlet case and of the "peculiar significance of every detail." He urged his colleagues, moreover, to shun "theories and assertions that conflict with the treaties and agreements, statutes and decided cases, and the voluminous documented facts." The result proved the wisdom of that advice. Mayor George E. Norvell of Tulsa and the late Dennis W. Bushyhead, throughout the years as associate attorneys also consistently supplied valuable contributions to the combined effort required to win the case against a formidable adversary. Co-author Earl Boyd Pierce, General Counsel of the Cherokee Nation, researched Cherokee history and prepared the first draft of the petition, was an associate attorney in the Outlet case, and spearheaded the lengthy litigation to final conclusion in 1973.

The United States apparently attempted to keep its word with respect to the promised accounting agreed to by the Jerome Commission in 1891. In 1893, it employed at its cost the nationally known firm of Slade and Bender, Certified Public Accountants of Akron, Ohio, who conducted the accounting in Washington, finishing it the following year. The accounting reflected an unpaid balance due the Cherokees under the Treaty of 1835 of $1,111,284.70 plus interest from June 12, 1838, until paid. By act of the national council, the tribe approved the accounting and forwarded to the Interior Department its request for an appropriation to pay the award by the Congress then in session.

On the pretext that the accountants had exceeded their authority, certain officers in the Department of Interior and a few Congressmen fomented a controversy over the question of the money due as interest. As a consequence, the Attorney General declined to approve the accountants' award. Then by non-action Congress participated in breaking the Outlet Agreement by failing to make immediate payment as expressly provided. Yet the land was gone and along with the disappointment of the nation's keenest and ablest leaders, these events broke the hearts of the Cherokee people.

The proposal continued, however, to linger in the Department of Interior. Eventually, it became involved in the question of whether the tribal government should be terminated to pave the way for statehood. In 1898, the Curtis Act approved an agreement with the Choctaws and Chickasaws and the Creeks for allotments in severalty in an effort to terminate tribal governments. Yet the Cherokees held out until July 1, 1902, when by tribal vote the Cherokee Allotment Agreement was ratified. The agreement permitted the Cherokees to sue in the U. S. Court of Claims to collect the debt due them under the Treaty of 1835 as determined by the accountants' report. Suit was eventually brought for the Eastern (Emigrant) Cherokees against the United States in the Court of Claims by Robert L. Owen and Frank J. Boudinot.

This suit met stout resistance from the Department of Justice. Yet the Cherokee attorneys knew that their case was sound and had carefully prepared it. After trial, judgement was entered in favor of the Cherokees in accordance with the Slade-Bender Accountants' Award. The court held that the Cherokees were due the sum of $1,111,284.70 which had not been paid to them in accordance with the terms of the 1835 treaty plus interest from June 14, 1838, until paid.

It seems almost amazing that the United States felt aggrieved with this decision. In appealing to the Supreme Court, however, the government attorneys allowed the usually placid Chief Justice Melville Fuller an opportunity to castigate with almost religious fervor the agents of the government for the treatment the Cherokees received in the Outlet sale. Quoting Justice Nott, Chief Justice Fuller said: "The

HOUSTON BENGE TEEHEE, 1874-1952, Cherokee Claims Attorney, Assistant Attorney General of Oklahoma, member of the Supreme Commission of Oklahoma, and Registrar of the United States Treasury. Thus, the name and signature of a Cherokee appeared on all United States federal notes and bonds in the period from 1915 to 1919.

W. W. HASTINGS, 1866-1938, Attorney General of the Cherokee Nation in Oklahoma, and nine-term member of the U.S. House of Representatives from Oklahoma. See page 91 for biography.

ADMIRAL J. J. "JOCKO" CLARK, 1893-1971, highest ranking person of American Indian descent in U. S. military history. Clark entered the Naval Academy in 1913, graduated in 1918. He became a Navy pilot in 1925, commanded the aircraft carrier *Yorktown* during World War II. He went into combat in World War I and II and Korea, and retired with four-star rank.

Cherokee Nation has parted with the land (the Cherokee Outlet), has lost the time within which it might have appealed to the Court, and has lost the right to bring the items which it regards as incorrectly or unjustly disallowed to judicial arbitrament, and the United States are placed in the position of having broken and evaded the letter and spirit of their agreement."

After a complete review of every treaty and statute provision relating to this debt, the Supreme Court affirmed the judgment against the United States in the amount of the Slade-Bender Award of $1,111,264.70 with interest from June 12, 1838. Aggregating more than six million dollars as of April 30, 1906, this sum represented the largest judgement the Court of Claims had at that time ever rendered in an Indian tribal claims case.

Notwithstanding this splendid court victory, the Cherokees soon faced a totally different but just as perplexing problem. In early 1908, the Bureau of Indian Affairs superintendent at Muskogee, Oklahoma, had requested advice from the Commissioner of Indian Affairs concerning ownership of the bed of the navigable portion of the Arkansas River in Oklahoma. At that time the superintendent had on his desk for consideration several proposed sand and gravel leases, profferred by local citizens and corporations. He also had a record showing official Cherokee riverbed leasing activity stretching back for twenty years before the government as trustee took over the nation's property. In response to this request in March, 1908, the superintendent was advised by Washington that

> The Arkansas river through its length in the Cherokee Nation is a navigable stream under the laws of the United States.
>
> Under the above-quoted holding of the court, it must be conceded that when the State of Oklahoma was created, its jurisdiction and ownership of the lands below highwater mark of all navigable streams within its boundaries, became absolute. In other words, when the United States conveyed by warranty deed the lands occupied by the Cherokees, Creeks, Choctaws, Chickasaws, and Seminoles, it did not convey ownership of the beds of navigable streams, but reserved them for the benefit of the future state within whose boundaries they would fall. Thus, the State of Oklahoma, on its creation, became absolute owner of the bed of the Arkansas River, and the Cherokee Nation is not entitled to royalty for any sand or gravel taken from the bed of that river since November 16, 1907.

Given the value of the river bed, the decision of the government was most adverse to the interest of the Cherokees. If they knew of the policy, tribal leaders — under attack for fifteen years and suffering from "a catalogue of woes" — apparently were too weary to resist it.

From that day until December, 1966, the policy of the Interior Department followed that set in 1908. No effort whatsoever was put forth to test the "grave" legal question concerning Indian title to the river bed. Moreover, the U. S. expended several millions of dollars on the over-all development of the Arkansas River for navigation and other purposes. Two hydroelectric power dams to cost over $200,000,000 were off the drawing boards and were in the course of construction, without consultation with the Cherokees.

The Cherokee General Counsel made a futile effort to negotiate with the State of Oklahoma the question of title and royalties due the tribe from sand, gravel and gas production. Upon discovering that the Departments of Interior and Justice would assume a neutral attitude, the Cherokee attorneys, Earl Boyd Pierce and Andrew C. Wilcoxen, entered suit in December, 1966. The attorneys asserted that all of the river bed above the mouth of the Canadian River to Muskogee and the north half below the Canadian to the Arkansas state line belonged to the Cherokee Nation. Their suit sought not only an accounting against the State of Oklahoma, sixteen oil companies, and two sand and gravel companies, but an injunction against interference with Cherokee possession of the property. After court dismissal of their suit naively claiming the entire navigable bed to

70

Muskogee, the Choctaw and Chickasaw Nations in mid-summer of 1967 intervened in the Cherokee suit against Oklahoma, *et al.*

After adverse decisions by the Federal District Court at Muskogee and the U. S. Court of Appeals at Denver, the landmark case ultimately reached the Supreme Court in Washington. Following repeated consultations and earnest persuasion by the Cherokee attorneys, the Interior and Justice Department attorneys eventually joined the Indian Nations in the litigation, and with much "vigor" aided the joint efforts. In 1970, the highest court finally made its ruling in a four-to-three classical decision. In an opinion written by Justice Thurgood Marshall and supported by an able and caustic concurring opinion by Justice William O. Douglas, it held that the 100 mile stretch of the navigable portion of the river from Ft. Smith, Arkansas, up to Muskogee, Oklahoma, belonged to the Cherokee, the Choctaw and Chickasaw Nations.

One wonders at the cost to the tribes of fifty-eight years of denial of their rights to the Arkansas River bed. The Cherokee Nation does not know today the extent of the benefits to which it is entitled. Anxious to assist the tribes in determining the value of and the damages resulting from the loss of this valuable property, Congress in 1972 appropriated $440,000 for the Bureau of Indian Affairs to make this determination. This legislation resulted, no doubt, in part from President Nixon's earlier admonition that the government had an obligation to develop U. S. Indian trust property and to avoid any conflicts of interest with the tribes. Serious questions are now before the Cherokees and the government regarding the nature, extent, and value of all property interests in the river bed. The nation is looking forward with considerable hope of settling these questions with finality. It may thus be observed that the Cherokees are at the threshold of a new relationship with the United States. Instead of resurrecting and asserting long dormant and almost forgotten treaty claims against the government, the tribe will strive to preserve for the benefit of all the Cherokee people its hard-won heritage.

The cost, for example, of the 17,000 acres the Cherokee Nation now owns and the $15,000 expended in the burial of indigent Cherokees since statehood were reimbursed to the federal government as offsets allegedly chargeable to the Outlet judgement of 1961. Chief Keeler recognized that such burial expense probably should have been borne by the respective counties as was the case with other deceased citizens. Yet the chief reasoned and so advised the attorneys that inasmuch as the government was to be reimbursed for the land purchased in the 1940's, the similar moral claim of the United States for the burial expense should likewise be paid. In the same spirit, Congress in 1968 permitted the Cherokees to repurchase 2,667 acres of their former domain at Chilocco for $3.75 per acre, the same price they had been paid for this immensely valuable wheat land. Future earnings from this tract are committed by an understanding between Chief Keeler and the Congress to the perpetual higher educational benefit of Cherokee fullblood children.

THE FUTURE

Strictly speaking, before the legal as distinguished from wholly moral claims arising from Cherokee relations with the federal and state government can be considered closed, three important items remain to be completed.

First, the river bed case is still in federal court, awaiting resolution of the inter-tribal boundary controversy by judicial decree. Congress has permitted the nations to submit to the judiciary their respective contentions on the title question covering the stretch of the river below the Canadian River where the Arkansas River forms the boundary between the Cherokee Nation on the north and the Choctaw Nation on the south. While the litigation progresses, the appraisal and evaluations of the damages resulting from the incorporation of the river bed into the extensive Arkansas River navigation project will be completed. Cherokee attorneys in this case, including Paul M. Niebell, Mike

Yaroschuk, Joseph Muskrat, Andrew Wilcoxen and Earl Boyd Pierce, are planning to appeal directly to Congress to redress the Cherokee claim for just compensation for the loss of all tribal property and property rights. It is their belief that because the Congress authorized the taking of tribal property, it should review the Department of Interior evaluations and fix the amount of damage.

Second, the land acreage accounting which the Jerome Commission refused in 1891 remains to be adjusted. In 1973, bills were introduced in both houses of Congress to pay the Cherokee Nation $13,000,000 for a recently discovered land shortage of 547,000 acres granted in the Cherokee Patent of 1838. This figure was unchallenged by the Interior Department after a recent two year review. Cherokee attorneys are satisfied that their computation will be found correct, and that Congress will act justly in the matter. Again, it is generally felt that the Cherokee Nation should not be required to resort to litigation which experience has proven to be expensive and time consuming.

Lastly, the Cherokee claim against the people and State of Texas requires attention. The detailed history of this obligation has received wide-spread publicity over the years and need not be repeated here. Renewed efforts to adjust the debt due the Cherokees and their associated bands have been commenced. Much hope abides that when the people of Texas come to know that their greatly celebrated patriots, particularly the most honorable and famous achiever of their liberty, President Sam Houston, pledged his solemn, written word and the honor of the Texas people that the Cherokee rights to their land in Texas would be protected, this 150 year old debt will be properly paid. The Cherokee faith in Sam Houston and in the people of Texas firmly supports this hope.

Cherokees generally, and their myriad of friends everywhere, are aware of the new revitalization programs inaugurated by Principal Chief Keeler. After 1907, the nation's land resources were practically nil, the treasury depleted, and the nation's governmental structure dismanteled save for the periodic appointment of a Principal Chief by the U. S. President. Federal programs to meet the dire needs of hundreds of fullblood families were scant, and due to diminishing congressional appropriations as well as a woeful lack of tribal organization, the over-all fullblood picture was pathetic.

Improvement of this situation began in the mid-forties when Chief Milam first lent a skilled hand to tribal organization. His concern inspired many Cherokees, including his successor, Principal Chief Keeler, to cooperate with the federal, state and local governments in finding solutions to the economic problems confronting large numbers of worthy Cherokees. The many practical programs which evolved to provide jobs convenient to the Cherokee communities, through the establishment of new industries and the Cherokee industrial-cultural center complex have proven most fruitful.

It seems appropriate in concluding this brief account of the Cherokee Nation's history to ponder a few thoughts from the mind of the currently elected leader of the Cherokee people. In the Masonic oration laying the cornerstone in the new Cherokee National Museum near Tahlequah on July 21, 1973, Principal Chief W. W. Keeler expressed very vividly and eloquently the heart and mind of the modern Cherokee:

"The ceremony in which we are taking part today is only a visible evidence of what we believe – that the heritage of a people is as important to their tomorrows as it is to their todays. . . .

"The Cherokee National Museum which we see under construction beside us is the physical embodiment of a dream. A dream that some day the story of the Cherokee people would be portrayed in such a manner that all the world would recognize the strengths and accomplishments of the Tribe. And it is a continuing part of that dream that all Cherokees, regardless of degree of blood or status in life, will come to realize the greatness of the Cherokee past, hold our heads high, and live up to the promises inherent in our heritage . . .

"And to future generations of Cherokees in particular, and to future generations of people everywhere, we of our generation charge them with continuing what we have started here — preservation of the continuing story of the Cherokee people to show that the past is not only prologue — as inscribed at the entrance of the National Archives in Washington — but a living dynamic thing of which each of us is an important part. For we are products of our past, as incoming generations will be products of what we are today . . .

"The nature and purpose of this building whose cornerstone has been laid in this historic ceremony is symbolized in the permanence of the steel and concrete and stone with which it is being built — a structure for the ages. It is a fitting tribute to the heritage of the great Cherokee Nation whose past, present and future will be stored within its walls."

"Restore, I pray you, to them, even this day, their lands, their vineyards, their oliveyards, and their houses, also the hundredth part of the money, and of the corn, the wine, and the oil, that ye exact of them."
— Nehemiah 5:11

CHEROKEE SEAL

The Cherokee National Council adopted the Seal of The Cherokee Nation on December 11, 1871. A seven-pointed star surrounded by an oak leaf wreath appears in the center of the seal. The seven-pointed star represents the seven ancient clans referred to in ritual songs sung in ancient tribal ceremonials. The oak leaf wreath symbolizes the courageous spirit of the people by recalling the live oak. This major hardwood timber of the Cherokee homeland was used to maintain the sacred fire perpetually burning in the town house at a central point in Cherokee territory.

The outside border of the seal bears the words "Seal of the Cherokee Nation" in English, followed by two words for "Cherokee Nation" in characters of the Sequoyah syllabary. These are pronounced "Tsa-la-gi-hi A-ye-li." At the lower edge of the seal appears the date when the constitution of the Cherokee Nation West was adopted, September 6, 1839.

This seal appeared on Cherokee Nation documents until the United States officially dissolved tribal government upon the admission of Oklahoma to the federal union.

— Adapted from Muriel H. Wright

BIOGRAPHIES OF
DISTINGUISHED CHEROKEES

There is no history, Emerson is quoted as saying, there is only biography. It is true that the story of the Cherokee people is reflected in the story of the remarkable achievements of individual Cherokees. Surely no people better illustrates the importance of personal achievement than the Cherokee. Not just one but two Cherokees represent the State of Oklahoma by statues in the Hall of Fame in the United States Capitol. Oklahoma's two choices were both Cherokees, men chosen from one relatively small and seemingly insignificant native Indian people. How many groups the size of the Cherokees can claim both a Sequoyah and a Will Rogers?

These biographies are themselves only representative and highly selective inasmuch as they include only a small number of the worthy Cherokees who might have been noted. There are others, hundreds if not thousands, in Cherokee history whose achievements are equally praiseworthy.

JOHN MARTIN

Few Cherokees were ever of greater service to their people than John Martin, one of the first and surely one of the most astute Cherokee lawyers. A man of considerable wealth, Martin belonged to a distinguished English family which early intermarried with the Cherokees. Martin held office as Judge of the Amohee District and Cooweescoowee District, Treasurer of the Cherokee Nation, Delegate to the Cherokee Constitutional Convention, and first Chief Justice of the Cherokee Nation.

John Martin is especially respected for his work as a delegate to the Cherokee Constitutional Convention in 1826-27 and for his work as a pioneer judge. The Martin place in Georgia was especially prosperous and the home he built there was most spacious. Reportedly, Martin at one time required 80 slaves to tend his farms and businesses, including a public house and a gin. He worked hard to protect the people of the Cherokee Nation from abuses by hostile white neighbors and attended important meetings in Washington designed to prevent removal and confiscation of Indian lands in the southeast. He emigrated to the west in 1837, served the Cherokees as Chief Judge of the Supreme Court in the new territory and died in 1840 in Fort Gibson, where he is buried.

JESSE BUSHYHEAD

Although never Chief of the Cherokee Nation, Jesse Bushyhead was probably the most influential Cherokee of his day: a minister, teacher, interpreter, civic and political leader, policeman, lawyer, Clerk of the National Council and Chief Justice of the Supreme Court. Indian Agent P. M. Butler described him as a "man of piety, decision, and intelligence." In a secret report, Ethan Allan Hitchcock advised that Bushyhead was a wise man whose support was necessary to gain acceptance among the Cherokees.

Among the distinguished ancestors of Bushyhead were Capt. John Stuart of the British Army, Lodovic Grant, Susannah Emory and Nancy Foreman. The family name was given to Capt. Stuart because of his bushy and wild colored hair. The Indian name *Oo-no-dutu* became translated as "Bushyhead."

Although slightly younger than Chief John Ross, Jesse Bushyhead provided wise counsel at the time of removal and directed Detachment Number 3 over the infamous "Trail of Tears." In his party of 950, only 38 died on the march, while six were born, including a daughter of Rev. and Mrs. Bushyhead. Perhaps more important than this achievement was his work to restore the spirit of the Cherokee people once the survivors settled in the west.

82

JOHN ROSS

Born in 1790 at Turkeytown in present Alabama, Ross was the grandson of a halfblood Cherokee woman, Ann Shorey, and a whiteman, John McDonald. Although himself only one-eighth Cherokee, Ross served as elected Chief longer than any in tribal history and was probably the most popular chief among the fullblood Cherokees.

From the time of a mission to the Cherokees in Arkansas in 1809 until his death in 1866, Ross devoted his life to public service. He was adjutant of the Cherokee regiment which fought with Andrew Jackson at the Battle of Horseshoe Bend and later served on the Cherokee Council and as President of the National Committee of the Cherokee Nation. He was President of the Cherokee Constitutional Convention of 1827 and became Chief in 1828. Ross remained Chief of the Cherokees from that time until his death in 1866 with the exception of a time when he was deposed by federal authorities during the Civil War.

Ross extended his influence beyond the boundaries of the Cherokee Nation. Ross always regarded Cherokee removal as a great personal failure. During his later years as Chief, the Cherokees entered what has been called their "Golden Age" and developed a sound economic, political and social system for his people.

Given the Cherokee name Killikeenah (Buck), Elias Boudinot took his English name out of gratitude for the assistance of a benefactor who helped educate him at the mission school in Cornwall, Connecticut. Like his cousin John Ridge, Boudinot married a daughter of New England and brought her to the Cherokee Nation in Georgia.

Boudinot became a minister, writer, newspaperman, translator and patriot. He edited the first Indian newspaper ever published in a native language, *The Cherokee Phoenix,* using the Sequoyah syllabary. Boudinot was of great value to Rev. Samuel Worcester in his work with the gospels. In the tradition of great newspapermen, Boudinet worked to build the little Indian newspaper into an important instrument of service to the tribe. He developed a strong editorial policy. Joining with others of similar persuasion, Boudinot signed the Treaty of New Echota in 1835, and was assassinated in the West.

The son and two grandsons of Elias Boudinot pictured on page 25 through the courtesy of the Boudinot family of Fort Gibson, Oklahoma, were all admitted to practice before the Supreme Court of the United States, theirs being the only family in the Cherokee Nation with this distinction.

GENERAL STAND WATIE

Stand Watie is best known as a Confederate general in the Civil War. Students of that war know as his biographer Mabel Washbourne Anderson notes that "General Watie had the honor of making the last surrender of the war, which occurred at Doaksville, in the Choctaw Nation, June 23, 1865, nearly three months after the surrender of General Lee."

The nature of this great Cherokee military hero is clearly recorded by his biographers. "He never ordered a charge that he did not lead, yet he never received a wound in battle. The fullbloods believed that he possessed a charmed life and no bullet was ever moulded that could kill him. His personal acts of courage furnish full foundation for this belief and his name stands for the very definition of bravery among his people today . . ."

Elias Boudinot's brother and also a leader in the removal party, Watie barely escaped assassination in 1839. Despite the many books written and perhaps being written or to be written on the pros and cons of the Cherokee Treaty of 1835, the authors here attest that the Cherokee signers, as well as their opponents, were totally honest, and they and their descendants remained fiercely loyal Cherokees, dedicated to the general welfare of all the Cherokee people regardless of party affiliation.

The transition of the Cherokee Nation from a people of clan revenge to a people of constitutional laws was made possible by men like Major Ridge. He and his brother Oo-Wa-Tee were Deer Clan members. As a fullblood, Cherokee-speaking member of the tribe, he exerted a powerful force in the adoption of early laws abolishing blood revenge and substituting the "lighthorse" or tribal police.

Major Ridge encouraged young Cherokees to seek an education at mission schools in the Cherokee Nation and in the East. He became a man of considerable wealth. The 1835 census of the State of Georgia reported that Ridge lived on an Oostenaulee River plantation with six half bloods and one fullblood member of his family and owned twenty-one slaves and two ferry boats.

Among other offices held by Ridge was that of Speaker of the Cherokee Council and of President of the Cherokee Committee. He was considered the leader of the "removal faction" of the Cherokees and signed the Treaty of New Echota of 1835. As author of an earlier law concerning the death penalty for selling tribal lands, he was aware of the risks, but thought resistance an impossible course. He was assassinated in Arkansas on June 22, 1839.

JOHN RIDGE

The tragedy of the political assassinations of leaders of the removal party and signers of the Treaty of New Echota of 1835 is no more clearly illustrated than in the death of the brilliant Cherokee scholar John Ridge. Born in 1803, Ridge was the son of the important and influential Major Ridge, and was carefully educated for tribal leadership.

Young Ridge attended school at Spring Place Mission and at the Cornwall Mission in Connecticut where he created quite a controversy when he fell in love with a very proper New England daughter named Sarah Bird Northrup. They were married in 1824 and she came to live with him.

Ridge exerted considerable personal influence in the Cherokee Nation when he was elected to the Cherokee National Council in 1824. Like most Cherokees, he fought Georgia's efforts to seize Cherokee land. Later, he joined with other members of his family as well as other prominent Cherokees including a brother of Chief John Ross in arguing for voluntary removal. He signed the Treaty of New Echota and soon migrated to the Cherokee Nation in the west. John Ridge was assassinated on June 22, 1839, along with his father, Major Ridge, and his cousin Elias Boudinot in a brutal emasculation of leadership and one of the most tragic events in Cherokee history.

JOHN ROLLIN RIDGE

Foremost among the literary men produced by the Cherokee Nation was John Rollin Ridge, pioneer author, newspaper editor, and poet laureate of California. His grandfather was Major Ridge and his father John Ridge. His life span, historian Carolyn Thomas Foreman notes, "carried him from a birthplace in the Eastern Cherokee Nation to his grave in California by way of Indian Territory and Arkansas."

By training a lawyer and by heritage a crusader, Ridge is best known as a poet and journalist. A fellow California editor concluded that "no California newspaper of any political persuasion was handled with more dignity or true, manly bearing" than Ridge's *Marysville National Democrat*. His most lasting work is a California adventure tale entitled *The Life and Adventures of Joaquin Murietta* written under his pen name "Yellow Bird." In print for more than a century since it was published in 1854, this volume is regarded as a classic.

Ridge wrote for a number of publications, including San Francisco's distinguished *Golden Era*. Among his fellow contributors to it were Bret Harte, Mark Twain, Joaquin Miller, Charles Warren Stoddard and Orpheus C. Kerr. Horace Greeley called Ridge "quite a poet" and "the handsomest man I ever saw."

WILL ROGERS

Beloved not only as an entertainer but also as a philosopher, Will Rogers seemed to understand what being an American meant and 'to appreciate both the strengths and weaknesses of this country. The wry, ironic sense of things which he possessed was an important part of the Cherokee heritage and the hallmark of this man who taught us to laugh at ourselves.

William Penn Adair Rogers was born November 4, 1879, on a ranch between Oologah and Claremore, and appeared on the 1880 census for the Cooweescoowee District of the Cherokee Nation. He was the son of Clement Vann Rogers and Mary Schrimpsher.

Rogers brought a glimpse of the frontier, the cowboy, the Indian and the Cherokee to the world in his varied career as a humorist, columnist, stage personality, motion picture actor, radio commentator, political analyist, world traveler, and friend to all mankind. The world was shocked when he died in an Alaskan plane accident in August of 1935. Bettie Blake Rogers, the lovely woman from Rogers, Arkansas, whom he had married in 1908, lost a devoted husband, and William Vann, Mary Amelia and James Blake Rogers a remarkable father. The world lost a man whose extraordinary talents had made him a world citizen with enduring influence.

One of the most respected and far sighted men to serve in the U. S. Senate was Robert L. Owen. As co-author of the Owen-Glass Bill, he was one father of the Federal Reserve System. The sound fiscal and banking policies which Owen fostered brought the United States into the modern financial world and enabled the federal government to survive the economic pressures of global economic warfare and increasing domestic needs.

A Cherokee of distinguished tribal ancestors, Owen prized a four-inch silver medal presented by President Thomas Jefferson to one of his maternal line, Thomas Chisholm, a Chief of the Western Cherokees. Owen himself was born February 2, 1856, in Lynchburg, Virginia, the son of Robert L. Owen, President of the Virginia and Tennessee Railroad, and Narcissa Clark Chisholm, a Cherokee.

Owen came to the Cherokee Nation soon after graduation from Washington and Lee University in about 1877 to teach in the Cherokee Orphan Asylum at Tahlequah. Later he became agent for the Five Civilized Tribes and in 1881 began to practice law. He organized the First National Bank of Muskogee and served as its president for ten years. He and Thomas P. Gore were chosen Oklahoma's two senators after statehood in 1907.

The life of W. W. Hastings spanned epochal changes in the Cherokee Nation. Born in 1866, he held office under the old Tribal Government structure, during the transition from tribe to statehood, and finally represented the citizens of the Second District of Oklahoma for nine terms in the U. S. House of Representatives. At the time of his voluntary retirement in 1934, Hastings was regarded as the most influential single figure in Congressional Indian programs.

Hastings grew to manhood on a farm at Beattie's Prairie, Delaware District, Cherokee Nation, attended the Cherokee Male Seminary and taught in the public schools of the Cherokee Nation. In 1889, he graduated from the Law Department of Vanderbilt University and returned to the Cherokee Nation, where he formed a law partnership with E. C. Boudinot II and W. P. Thompson. He served the Cherokee Nation as delegate to many conferences and hearings before federal government agencies in Washington, Attorney General of the Cherokee Nation, Superintendent of Education for the Cherokees, and Adviser to the Chiefs.

After the end of tribal government, Hastings was Attorney for the Cherokee Nation in making final rolls, allotment of lands, and cases before the Court of Claims and the Supreme Court of the United States.

91

JACK AND ANNA KILPATRICK

The literary, musical and historical tradition of the Cherokees bloomed in the work of the Cherokee husband-and-wife team of Jack and Anna Gritts Kilpatrick. The late Jack Kilpatrick was one of America's most distinguished authors, educators, musical composers, linguists and folklorists. His work was so significant that the Cherokee Nation presented him a special medallion thought to be the only such award given since Sequoyah was so honored.

Dr. Kilpatrick served many years on the faculty at Southern Methodist University. During that time, he composed hundreds of original works including musical scores for the Cherokee dramas *Unto These Hills* and *The Trail of Tears*. He was widely regarded at the time of his death as one of the country's most distinguished composers and talented native American musicians.

Equally important is the work which he and his wife completed together. They collected important Cherokee language documents, taped lengends, chants, and other traditional native Cherokee language oral materials. Included among their many published books were *Friends, of Thunder, The Shadow of Sequoyah,* and *New Echota Letters.* Anna, a descendant of Sequoyah, served as a professor at Northeastern State College after Jack's death.

JACK GREGORY

Distinguished among the contemporary writers and educators produced by the Cherokee Nation is the author, folklorist, and humorist Jack Gregory. Following in the steps of Cherokee ancestors from the West, Starr, Thompson, Fields, and Foreman families, Gregory has explored the traditions of the Cherokee people and written and lectured extensively on his tribal lore and history. He has edited or co-authored fifteen books and has served on the faculty of the University of Arkansas and is currently a professor at the University of West Florida. Gregory's recent work has been in intercultural communication and Indian education. In 1971-1972, he was a Ford Foundation Fellow at Arizona State University. He is the only Cherokee to have served as a member of the Tribal Council of the Eastern Creeks, a position to which he was elected while working as a consultant on the Indian Oral History Project of the Doris Duke Foundation.

Among Gregory's notable publications are *Cherokee Spirit Tales, Choctaw Spirit Tales, Creek-Seminole Spirit Tales, Sam Houston with the Cherokees,* and the *Cherokee Cookbook.*

MARIE L. WADLEY, a Cherokee and Shawnee, who served in the Muskogee office of the Bureau of Indian Affairs over 42 years. She was Executive Secretary for the Inter-Tribal Council of the Five Civilized Tribes for nearly 20 years, and first President of the Board of Directors of the Five Civilized Tribes Museum. She served the Cherokee Tribe in a wide variety of offices, and has been active in philanthropic, professional, social and religious activities.

SUGGESTED READINGS

ABEL, ANNIE H. *The American Indian under Reconstruction*. Cleveland: Arthur H. Clark Co., 1925.

A scholarly, well-documented account of the 1866 Ft. Smith Conference and negotiations in Washington.

BASS, ALTHEA. *Cherokee Messenger*. Norman: University of Oklahoma Press, 1936.

A biography of the most important missionary to serve the Cherokees, Rev. Samuel A. Worcester.

BROWN, JOHN P. *Old Frontiers*. Kingsport: n. p., 1938.

The Cherokees before resettlement West.

CHEROKEE NATION. *Constitution and Laws of the Cherokee Nation*. Parsons, Kansas: Cherokee Nation, 1893.

Suggests the governmental attainments of the Cherokees.

FOREMAN, GRANT. *Indian Removal*. Norman: University of Oklahoma Press, 1932.

A documented historical study of the removal controversy and the Trail of Tears based upon governmental and tribal records.

95

—— *The Five Civilized Tribes.* Norman: University of Oklahoma Press, 1934.

Life among the Five Civilized Tribes, including the Cherokees, in the period after removal.

GABRIEL, RALPH HENRY. *Elias Boudinot, Cherokee and His America.* Norman: University of Oklahoma Press, 1941.

An interesting biography of one of the most important and controversial individuals in Cherokee history.

GREGORY, JACK AND RENNARD STRICKLAND. *Cherokee Spirit Tales: Tribal Myths, Legends, and Folklore.* Fayetteville, Arkansas: Indian Heritage Association, 1969.

Willard Stone illustrates this limited edition collection of Cherokee tribal tales.

—— *Sam Houston with the Cherokees.* Austin: University of Texas Press, 1967.

A picture of Sam Houston and his life with the Western Cherokees in the era before the Trail of Tears.

HITCHCOCK, ETHAN ALLEN. *A Traveler in Indian Territory.* Edited by Frant Foreman. Cedar Rapids, Iowa; Torch Press, 1930.

A very favorable picture of the Cherokee

Nation in both official and unofficial accounts of a prominent visitor.

KILPATRICK, JACK AND ANNA G. KILPATRICK. *New Echota Letters: Contributions of Samuel A. Worcester to the Cherokee Phoenix.* Dallas: Southern Methodist University Press, 1968.

Reprinted materials on social, political, linguistic, and religious aspects of Cherokee culture from the official Cherokee tribal newspaper.

MALONE, HENRY T. *Cherokees of the Old South.* Athens: University of Georgia Press, 1956.

Single most valuable book on Cherokees prior to removal.

MOONEY, JAMES. *Myths of the Cherokees.* Washington: Nineteenth Annual Report, Bureau of American Ethnology, 1900.

This is considered the starting point for any serious student of Cherokee tribal history.

ROYCE, CHARLES C. *The Cherokee Nation of Indians.* Washington: Fifth Annual Report, Bureau of American Ethnology, 1887.

A precise, detailed, and important study of the Cherokee people, especially tribal dealings with the U. S. government.

STARR, EMMET. *Starr's History of the Cherokees.* Edited by Jack Gregory and Rennard Strickland. Fayetteville, Arkansas: Indian Heritage Association, 1968.

Considered the authority on Cherokee family history.

WARDELL, MORRIS L. *A Political History of the Cherokee Nation.* Norman: University of Oklahoma Press, 1938.

An overview which traces important developments in tribal government from removal to statehood.

WILKINS, THURMAN. *Cherokee Tragedy.* New York: Macmillan, 1970.

One of the very best books ever written on the dilemma of the Cherokees as seen in the struggles of the Ridge family.

WOODARD, GRACE S. *The Cherokees.* Norman: University of Oklahoma Press, 1963.

Cherokee tribal history written from the viewpoint of the Ross faction.

WRIGHT, MURIEL H. *A Guide to the Indian Tribes of Oklahoma.* Norman: University of Oklahoma Press, 1951.

Recognized as the "Bible" by scholars and students of the Indian Nations and Tribes in Oklahoma.

THE AUTHORS

 EARL BOYD PIERCE, General Counsel of the Cherokees, is an enrolled member of the Tribe (M-2609) who aided Chief Keeler in launching current Cherokee revitalization programs. A lawyer (LL.B., University of Oklahoma), Pierce belongs to the Oklahoma, Federal, and American Bar Associations, American Trial Lawyers Association, and the American Judicature Society. He is licensed to practice before U. S. Courts, including the Court of Claims and the Supreme Court. Before serving as associate counsel in Cherokee cases discussed in this book, Pierce worked in Washington in the Department of the Interior and Department of Justice. A member of the Board of Directors of the Oklahoma Historical Society, the Cherokee National Historical Society, and the Cabinet of the Cherokee Nation, Pierce has lectured extensively on tribal history and researched for fifty years the major archives for evidence in Cherokee cases. "But for the steadfast devotion of my wife, Ruth, and daughter, Mrs. Harry M. Shytles, Jr., I think I might have given up on our long, complex, and unending Cherokee struggles," Pierce notes.

RENNARD STRICKLAND, College of Law, The University of Tulsa, has written extensively on Indian law, policy and culture. A Fellow in Legal History of the American Bar Foundation, he holds the B.A. from Northeastern State College, an M.A. from the University of Arkansas, and the J.D. and S.J.D. from the University of Virginia. Strickland previously taught at the University of Arkansas, University of West Florida, and St. Mary's University. He has carried out fieldwork among Southeastern Indian Tribes, including participation in the Duke Foundation Indian Oral History project. Among his other books are two listed in the "Suggested Readings" and *Fire and the Spirits: Cherokee Law from Clan to Court.*

In recognition of his service to Indian people, Professor Strickland has been awarded the sacred sash of the Creek Chiefs.

"Trying to distill the essence of the Cherokee people and their history into this brief and impressionistic portrait has been an exciting and challenging experience," Strickland observes.